TREASURY OF LITERATURE
UNIT HOLISTIC READING ASSESSMENT
TEACHER'S EDITION
GRADE 6

SENIOR AUTHOR

ROGER C. FARR

HARCOURT
BRACE

Orlando Atlanta Austin Boston San Francisco Chicago Dallas New York
Toronto London

ISBN 0-15-305462-X

2 3 4 5 6 7 8 9 10   073   97   96   95   94

Contents

The Benefits of Assessment and Evaluation

by Roger C. Farr

The assessment and evaluation plan that accompanies any instructional program should be comprehensive and holistic, and it must focus on the needs of students, teachers, and others who help to plan and support a child's learning. The goal must be to provide useful and timely information and to support learning and teaching.

The primary group to benefit from evaluation is students. If students are to become effective readers and writers, they must be encouraged to accept responsibility for their own learning, becoming good judges and self-assessors of the effectiveness of their own reading and writing.

Teachers are the second group to be served by evaluation. Effective teachers have always based their instructional planning on classroom observations, students' reading and writing samples, and conversations with students. Test results, when they are used effectively, should be only one part of a more comprehensive picture.

The third group to be served by evaluation includes parents, school administrators, and community leaders concerned with students' literacy development. These groups all want to know how they can help children become effective readers and writers. They are interested not only in numbers derived from one-time test administrations, but they also want to know whether students are going to be able to read and write well enough to meet academic, vocational, and citizenship requirements.

An effective assessment and evaluation program must be carefully designed and developed to focus on and meet the needs of students, teachers, and others. The evaluation must be comprehensive, holistic, ongoing, similar to instruction, and integrated within the instructional program. These general goals could not possibly be achieved by any single component or instrument. However, all of the criteria can be met by a total assessment and evaluation program.

The assessment and evaluation program in *Treasury of Literature* has been developed to address each of the important aspects identified above. It includes a variety of tools to help teachers and students gain insights into students' literacy development on an ongoing basis. It provides teachers with choices; they can use any or all of the tools to meet instructional needs and to help their students become effective readers and writers. The variety of assessment and evaluation tools in *Treasury of Literature* provide opportunities to place students at their instructional levels, to assess the skills and strategies that reflect the instruction that research has shown is vital to learning to read and to write, to require students to read and integrate information for identifying or forming appropriate responses, and to allow students to rely on all aspects of language—listening, speaking, reading, and writing to construct responses.

Assessment and Evaluation in Treasury of Literature

TYPE OF ASSESSMENT	TREASURY OF LITERATURE COMPONENT
PORTFOLIO ASSESSMENT Combine product and process assessment in a comprehensive ongoing record of individual student's literacy development	**Portfolio Assessment Teacher's Guide** Suggestions and strategies for initiating, maintaining and evaluating a collection of each student's reading and writing activities; guidelines and suggestions for scheduling portfolio conferences, for using portfolio contents for teacher-student literacy conferences, and for discussing students' literacy development with parents, other teachers, and administrators
READING-WRITING PERFORMANCE ASSESSMENT Reading and writing performance tasks to determine whether students can use reading to write and whether they can accomplish a specific task	**Unit Integrated Performance Assessment** Six reading and writing prompts correlated to units in the student anthologies. These structured reading-writing tasks use authentic literature and are designed as models of realistic reading and writing activities in the instructional program and in the students' everyday lives.
HOLISTIC READING COMPREHENSION Criterion-referenced tests to assess vocabulary and comprehension in a global and holistic manner	**Unit Holistic Reading Assessment** Fiction and nonfiction passages accompanied by multiple-choice questions that focus on application of literal, inferential, and critical thinking. Passages are correlated to theme and content in student anthologies and are preceded by a purpose for reading which helps students focus on the passage. Optional sections include open-ended writing prompts and Self-assessment Surveys.
READING SKILLS ASSESSMENT Multiple-choice tests that measure students' mastery of major skills and strategies	**Unit Reading Skills Assessment** Multiple-choice tests to assess progress and diagnose students' specific needs in the major skills and strategies of decoding, vocabulary, comprehension, literary appreciation, and study skills taught in the program

ADVANTAGES	HOW OFTEN USED
Portfolio Assessment is comprehensive and should be integrated with instruction. The Portfolio Assessment Teacher's Guide is a resource that explains and models how to use portfolios in the classroom. It answers the questions about what goes in a portfolio, who is responsible for deciding what should be placed in a portfolio, how portfolios enhance instruction, and how a teacher can use a portfolio for assessment and evaluation and conferences.	Continuously throughout the school year. The Portfolio Assessment Teacher's Guide is a resource that teachers will use on an ongoing basis.
Integrated Performance Assessment prompts provide a natural, holistic assessment of realistic literacy activities. Students read and respond in writing to authentic children's literature. In addition to providing model papers to determine a reading score and a writing score, the Teacher's Edition also provides suggestions for informal observation of students' listening and speaking abilities.	Provided for use at the end of each unit of instruction
An easy-to-use and comprehensive assessment of students' progress in major reading comprehension objectives. In addition, options include open-ended responses and multiple-choice and free-response questions to help students learn to reflect on their interests and growth as readers. The teacher's edition provides model papers and specific directions for scoring and interpreting students' responses.	Provided for use at the end of each unit of instruction
An easy-to-use and comprehensive assessment of students' strengths and weaknesses in decoding, vocabulary, comprehension, literary appreciation, and study skills in a variety of formats that complement instruction.	Provided for use at the end of each unit of instruction

TYPE OF ASSESSMENT	*TREASURY OF LITERATURE* COMPONENT

LANGUAGE SKILLS AND WRITING ASSESSMENT

Multiple-choice and open-ended questions to assess students' mastery of language skills and writing prompts to determine students' ability to complete a writing form for a specific task, audience, and purpose

Unit Language and Writing Assessment

This two-part test is designed to provide information about students' knowledge of language skills and their ability to use the writing process to produce a writing sample. Part one presents six writing prompts which address task, audience, and purpose and cite primary traits of specific writing forms. The second part provides six writing scenarios accompanied by multiple-choice and open-ended questions to assess students' knowledge of grammar, mechanics, and usage in context.

PLACEMENT — GROUP

Information for placing students in the appropriate level of the program to assure that each student experiences maximum success as he or she begins instruction

Group Placement Test

Group-administered multiple-choice reading comprehension and vocabulary tests designed to provide valid placement information

PLACEMENT — INDIVIDUAL

Information for placing an individual student in the appropriate level of the program and diagnostic information about an individual student's strengths and weaknesses in reading and writing

Individual Inventory for Reading and Writing

This two-part resource for working with individual students includes a Placement Inventory for assessing comprehension and determining valid placement. The Diagnostic Inventory includes materials and directions for administering and interpreting miscue analysis (running record) and oral and written retellings as well as phonemic awareness and decoding skills to diagnose a student's strengths and weaknesses in reading and writing.

INFORMAL ASSESSMENT

Provides teachers with a means to determine which students are having difficulty — at a point when meaningful help can be given — without waiting until end-of-unit assessment

Informal Assessment Notes

Highlighted within the Teacher's Editions are point-of-use suggestions, strategies, and procedures for conducting informal student observation. Also, the Portfolio Assessment Teacher's Guide includes suggestions for using checklists, anecdotal records, students' work samples, and teacher-student conferences as part of the informal assessment procedures.

Provide point-of-use suggestions for student-directed strategies to help students reflect on and monitor their own learning and habits

Student Self-Assessment Notes

Highlighted within the Teacher's Editions are point-of-use student-directed suggestions to help students reflect on and monitor their own reading, writing, and learning.

Harcourt Brace School Publishers • Unit Holistic Reading Assessment

ADVANTAGES	HOW OFTEN USED
Comprehensive holistic assessment of writing and language skills. Writing prompts include a graphic organizer to support prewriting and drafting and self-directed questions for revising and proofreading. Self evaluation and peer evaluation checklists are also provided. Writing scenarios provide the context for open-ended and multiple-choice questions to assess students' knowledge and application of grammar, mechanics, and usage.	Provided for use at the end of each unit of instruction
Comprehensive and valid for determining if students can successfully read at particular levels of the program. Can be administered to an entire class.	Administered when the program is first begun. It may also be administered when new students arrive at a school.
Passages in two formats supported by suggestions in the Teacher's Edition may be used to conduct a miscue analysis (running record) or oral or written retellings to diagnose an individual's strengths and weaknesses in reading and writing as well as to resolve questions about an individual student's placement.	When making a placement decision for an individual student or when additional diagnostic information about an individual student is needed
Suggestions, strategies, and procedures appear at point of use so teachers can take advantage of the "teachable moment" to learn about a student's progress or recording student observations.	Woven throughout the instructional units and should be used continually throughout the instructional program
Point-of-use notes that encourage students to monitor and reflect on their reading and writing so that they can begin to take responsibility for their own improvement	Woven throughout the instructional units and should be used continually throughout the instructional program

5

Unit Holistic Reading Assessment

Description of the Test

The *Unit Holistic Reading Assessment* is a criterion-referenced test. The primary purpose of this assessment component is to provide specific information about each student's ability to perform tasks so that appropriate instructional decisions can be made.

This test assesses vocabulary and comprehension in a global and holistic manner and helps you to know if a student can adequately read at the level of ***Treasury of Literature*** being taught.

In addition, to assess students' abilities to respond in writing to reading in a variety of formats, optional open-ended items have been included with each passage.

Multiple-choice Items

A series of fiction and nonfiction reading passages have been selected to match the various reading levels of the program. Many of the passages have been taken from children's and adolescent literature and reflect the trend to use longer, more authentic reading selections to assess comprehension. There are two reading passages for each unit. Each reading passage is preceded by a "purpose for reading" that helps students to focus on the passage. Following each reading passage are eight multiple-choice reading comprehension questions. These questions assess literal, inferential, and critical thinking. There are sixteen reading comprehension questions for each unit of the program.

Optional Open-ended Items

Students are asked to provide written responses to one open-ended item at the end of each reading passage (two open-ended items per unit). These items assess students' abilities to use higher-order thinking skills such as synthesizing, extending, applying, comparing/contrasting, empathizing, visualizing, or selecting.

Each open-ended item is to be completed immediately after the passage is read. Students may work at their own pace when responding to an item and can then move on to the next reading passage. Model student papers and specific directions for scoring the responses are included in this booklet.

Optional Self-assessment Survey

An optional Self-assessment Survey is provided for each unit of the *Unit Holistic Reading Assessment*. The Self-assessment Survey is comprised of a combination of multiple-choice and free-response items. The purpose of the survey is to encourage students to think about the unit they have just completed and to reflect on the progress they are making as readers. Some of the items on the survey assess students' interests in and attitudes toward the unit just completed (e.g., "Were the stories in this unit interesting?"). Other items ask students to be more reflective about their own abilities and progress (e.g., "Did you have trouble understanding the stories in this unit?" "Are you becoming a more interested reader?").

Harcourt Brace School Publishers • Unit Holistic Reading Assessment

General Test Considerations

Before Getting Started

The following suggestions will help to provide valid and reliable assessment.

1. Be thoroughly familiar with the *Unit Holistic Reading Assessment* before beginning to administer the test. One way to become familiar with any test is to administer the test to yourself to alert you to any procedural difficulties your students may encounter.

2. Attempt to seat the students so that you can easily observe them. This will help you not only determine if students are on the correct page when the tests are started but also see that they mark answers to the items appropriately.

3. Be sure that each student has a pencil to mark responses and has written his or her name on the front of the test booklet.

4. Have on hand a demonstration copy of a student booklet as well as the directions for administering the test found in this manual. The general directions to the examiner are printed in regular type. The specific directions to be read aloud to the students are printed in *italic* type.

Scheduling the Test

It is suggested that each unit test be administered in one sitting. The *Unit Holistic Reading Assessment* is not a timed test. Most students will be able to complete the two reading passages and accompanying questions in approximately thirty to forty-five minutes. If your students complete the test before the allotted time, you may end the testing session. However, if you find some students need more time to complete all of the test items, allow them to keep working.

Specific Test Directions

Directions for the Multiple-choice Items

Prior to administering the unit test, read the following general directions to students:

Say: *We are going to take a test to find out how well you can read. Some of the questions will be easy and some will be more difficult. Do your very best and try to answer each of the questions.*

Write each student's name on a booklet before distributing the test booklets, or, if you prefer, distribute the booklets and have students write in their names. When administering the test, speak in a natural tone, pacing directions so that all students have time to answer. Repeat or clarify items that students do not hear or directions that they do not understand, but do not permit such explanations to reveal any answers. Directions that should be read verbatim to students are printed in *italic* type. Directions that are for your information only (not to be read to students) are printed in regular type.

Say: *Open your test booklet to page 1 and fold back the page so that you see only page 1.*

Make sure that each student has the correct page.

Harcourt Brace School Publishers • Unit Holistic Reading Assessment

Tell students to read the directions to themselves as you read them aloud:

Read each story and the questions that follow. Fill in the answer circle in front of the correct answer for each question.

Say: *You are to read two passages and the questions that follow. You will fill in the answer circle in front of the correct answer for each question. You may look back at the passages to help you choose your answers. As you read the two passages, you may notice some underlined words. There will be questions later about what those words mean. When you answer a question about the meaning of a word, you might want to look back in the passage and find the underlined word. Then you can better understand the meaning it has in that passage. When you have finished reading both passages and answering the questions that follow, put your pencil down and sit quietly until I tell you what to do next. Does everyone understand what you are to do?*

Provide help for any student who has difficulty.

Say: *You may begin now.*

Check to make sure everyone is on the right beginning page. As students begin to work, circulate to make sure that they are marking answers correctly and are completing the questions related to both passages.

Allow enough time for students to complete their reading and the test items.

Directions for the Optional Open-ended Items

If you are having the students complete the optional open-ended items, give the following directions. You might wish to have extra lined paper on hand for students who choose to write longer responses.

Say: *The last question after each passage is different. Turn to the last question at the end of the first passage in your booklet.*

Demonstrate with a test booklet. Tell students the correct page to turn to, and show an example of an open-ended item. Circulate to make sure all students have turned to the correct page.

Say: *The last question after each passage asks you to write your answer. You are to answer the question as soon as you have finished all the multiple-choice questions for that passage. There is space provided for you to write your answer. Do your best to answer the question, but do not be overly concerned about spelling or handwriting. If you want to use a word that you do not know how to spell, just try to spell the word as best you can. You will not be graded on your handwriting or spelling; you will be graded on what you write. Do the best job you can. Does everyone understand what you are to do?*

Provide help for any student who has difficulty.

If you wish to read each of the open-ended items aloud and explain them or elaborate

Harcourt Brace School Publishers ● Unit Holistic Reading Assessment

on what is required, feel free to do so. Do not give students any ideas for how to respond to the items, however.

Allow the students as much time as you think appropriate for completing the test questions. When students begin work on the first open-ended item, walk around the room, checking to make sure they are writing their answers in the correct space and that they understand the task.

Directions for the Optional Self-assessment Survey

If you are having the students complete the optional Self-assessment Survey, give the following directions. Students may write on the back of the booklets if extra space is needed.

Say: *The last thing I would like you to do is answer the questions on the Self-assessment Survey. This is not part of the test. There are no right or wrong answers to these questions. These questions will help you think about the unit we have just completed. These questions will also help you think about the progress you are making as a reader. Answer the questions honestly by explaining how you feel. Your answers will not affect your score on this test or your grade.*

Make certain that you explain to students that the Self-assessment Survey pertains to the unit they just completed in *Treasury of Literature* and not just the passages in the test booklet. You may want to remind students of the selections they read in the unit.

If you wish to read each of the questions aloud and explain them, feel free to do so. The Self-assessment Survey is designed to assess students' attitudes, interests, and self-awareness, not their reading ability.

Scoring and Interpreting

Multiple-choice Items

Each of the multiple-choice test items is scored 1 point if the answer is correct. If the answer is incorrect or left blank, 0 points are given. Thus, a perfect score would be 16. The answer keys for the multiple-choice items can be found later in this booklet. The open-ended items are optional and should be scored separately. Scores for the multiple-choice items should be interpreted as follows:

SCORE	INTERPRETATION	TEACHING SUGGESTIONS
15–16	Very good reader at this level of the program	Students scoring at this level should have no difficulty moving forward in the program.
13–14	Average reader at this level of the program	Students scoring at this level may need a little extra help.
11–12	Fair reader at this level of the program	Students scoring at this level may need more help. Other samples of students' performance should be examined to confirm their progress and pinpoint instructional needs.
10 or fewer	Poor reader at this level of the program	Students scoring at this level will almost certainly have difficulty completing this level of the program.

As with all tests, it is important not to place too much faith in a single test. The *Unit Holistic Reading Assessment* is only one sample of a student's reading. This sample of behavior should be compared to the information you have gathered from daily observations, work samples, and perhaps other test scores. The analytic scores provided by the *Unit Reading Skills Assessment* will provide valuable diagnostic information.

Optional Open-ended Items

A general scoring rubric has been designed to facilitate the scoring of the open-ended questions. A "scoring rubric" is a guide to assist in evaluating student responses. Look over the rubric (Figure 1) for a few moments. It is divided into three

Harcourt Brace School Publishers • Unit Holistic Reading Assessment

parts, representing the range of scores assigned to the open-ended items. A 3-point scale, ranging from a low of 1 to a high of 3, is used for scoring these items. A score of 3 can be thought of as "excellent" comprehension; a score of 2 as "adequate"; and a score of 1 as "unsatisfactory" comprehension.

The scoring rubric includes multiple features that need to be considered when determining a student's score. All features should be considered separately and then balanced thoughtfully. A response may or may not meet *all* of the criteria listed for a given score point. For example, a response may have *most* of the characteristics of a "3," but *some* of the characteristics of a "2." In such a situation, the response would receive a score of "3." You should approach the scoring holistically, weighing and balancing different aspects of the student's response. The model papers illustrate the score points for each open-ended item.

To apply the rubric, you will make an overall judgment about the student's degree of success in answering the open-ended item with a focused, well-developed response characterized by clear understanding of ideas in the reading passage. Questions such as the following can be used to guide your evaluation:

- **Does the response appropriately answer the question?**

- **Does the response reflect a clear understanding of ideas in the passage?**

- **When appropriate, has the student included ideas or information from the passage in the response? If so, is the information accurate?**

- **Has the student interpreted passage ideas in light of his or her prior knowledge or experience?**

General Rubric for Scoring Open-ended Items

How well did the student comprehend?

SCORE	CHARACTERISTICS
3	The student's comprehension is **excellent.** The response may— • clearly address the task • reflect a high degree of comprehension • show strong evidence of higher-order thinking • show strong evidence of using prior knowledge and experience in interpreting the passage • include substantial development and elaboration
2	The student's comprehension is **adequate.** The response may— • attempt to address the task • reflect a moderate degree of comprehension • show some evidence of higher-order thinking • show some evidence of using prior knowledge and experience in interpreting the passage • include limited development and elaboration
1	The student's comprehension is **unsatisfactory.** The response may— • fail to address the task • reflect a minimal degree of comprehension or a serious misunderstanding • show little or no evidence of higher-order thinking • show little or no evidence of using prior knowledge and experience in interpreting the passage • include little or no development and elaboration
NS	The student's response is **nonscorable.**

Figure 1

Harcourt Brace School Publishers ● Unit Holistic Reading Assessment

Remember that the open-ended items are intended to assess reading comprehension, not writing performance. Writing ability can be more appropriately assessed by using the *Unit Integrated Performance Assessment.*

To guide you further in evaluating student responses to the open-ended items, illustrative model papers are provided in this booklet. By reading and becoming familiar with these model papers, you can better understand how to apply the scoring rubric.

You may find that some responses are so far off the topic or are so badly written that they cannot be scored. Those responses should be marked **NS** (nonscorable) and should be put aside for further analysis at a later time. You must decide what constitutes a response that cannot be scored. Do so consistently for every student in your class. Some suggestions as to what might make a response nonscorable follow:

- **gibberish** (The writing is totally incoherent. You might want to ask the student to read it to you so that you might learn what he or she is trying to communicate.)

- **no writing, or only one or two words** (Is this typical of the student? If so, why? Is there a reason the student cannot produce a written response?)

- **verbatim copying** (The student has copied word for word from the reading passage and produced no original writing.)

In summary, follow these procedures when scoring the open-ended items:

1. Reread the reading passage and the open-ended item so that you are completely familiar with the task students were asked to complete.

2. Review the General Rubric for Scoring Open-ended Items.

3. Read and become familiar with the model papers supplied in this booklet.

4. Quickly scan through your class set of papers to get a feel for the range of the responses.

5. Read each individual student paper; use the General Rubric and the model papers to determine the score you feel the paper should receive.

Optional Self-assessment Survey

The Self-assessment Survey is intended to provide useful information about students' interests, attitudes, and awareness of their progress in reading. The items on the survey should not be scored as part of the test. Rather, you should review students' responses to gain insights into their ability to self-assess and monitor their own progress. Questions such as the following should guide your review:
- Are students able to engage in meaningful self-assessment?
- Are students demonstrating positive attitudes and interest toward reading?
- Do students recognize the progress they are making as readers?

Analyzing Student Performance

Each open-ended item is designed to emphasize higher-order thinking skills such as synthesizing, applying, empathizing, making value judgments, and extending.

Harcourt Brace School Publishers ● Unit Holistic Reading Assessment

Valuable insights into a student's ability to tap these thinking skills can be gained by evaluating the student's written response to each item.

You may find that some students are less successful in responding to open-ended items than in answering the multiple-choice items. This may occur for a number of reasons:

- The open-ended items are designed to elicit diverse responses. Some students might feel uncomfortable in approaching such a broad-based task when they are more accustomed to close-ended tasks that call for providing one correct answer. The students might lack the confidence and strategies necessary for structuring the task and formulating an original response.

- Some students may lack expertise in expressing ideas in written form. Such factors as limited vocabulary, poor organizational skills, lack of experience in supporting a viewpoint through examples and details, or little previous experience with creative writing could result in a weak response to an open-ended item. These same students might perform more successfully if responding orally or in a short-answer format.

- Some students, unaccustomed to tasks of this nature, might not clearly understand what they are to do.

- It is possible for students to have good comprehension on a literal level but to experience frustration when called upon to apply and use ideas from the reading.

Alternatively, you might find that some students experience a high degree of success when responding to the open-ended items but perform less successfully when responding in the multiple-choice format. A number of explanations are possible for this:

- Some students might grasp the global meaning of a passage while overlooking some of the supporting details presented.

- Some students might lack the test-taking skills necessary for success in answering certain kinds of questions (e.g., looking back for specific information or using context clues).

- A student might view items from an unusual individual viewpoint that results in missing the obvious correct answer. There might be an element of validity to the unique viewpoint, but there is no forum for explaining this in the close-ended, multiple-choice format.

As you read through your students' work, remember that your judgment is necessary in analyzing the open-ended responses. After analyzing a few papers, the task will become easier. Teacher judgment has proved to be insightful, useful, and consistent in assessing reading comprehension through writing.

Harcourt Brace School Publishers • Unit Holistic Reading Assessment

Reduced and Annotated Pupil Facsimile Pages

SHADES OF GOLD

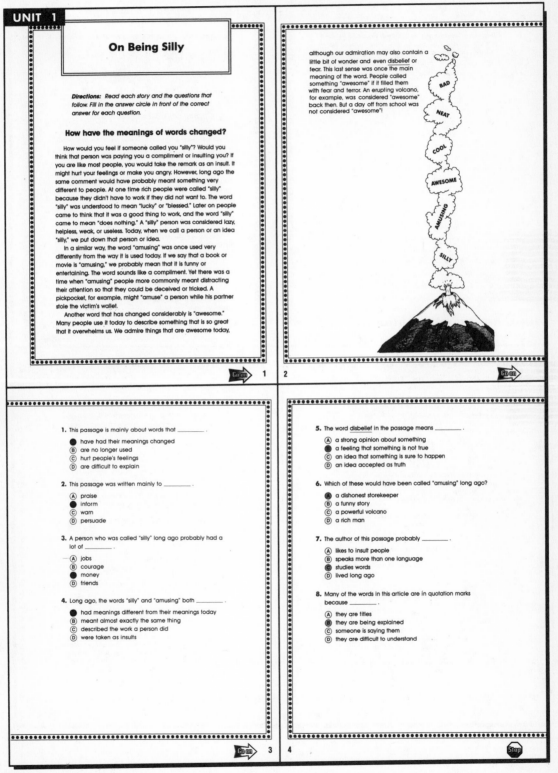

UNIT 1

On Being Silly

Directions: *Read each story and the questions that follow. Fill in the answer circle in front of the correct answer for each question.*

How have the meanings of words changed?

How would you feel if someone called you "silly"? Would you think that person was paying you a compliment or insulting you? If you are like most people, you would take the remark as an insult. It might hurt your feelings or make you angry. However, long ago the same comment would have probably meant something very different to people. At one time rich people were called "silly" because they didn't have to work if they did not want to. The word "silly" was understood to mean "lucky" or "blessed." Later on people came to think that it was a good thing to work, and the word "silly" came to mean "does nothing." A "silly" person was considered lazy, helpless, weak, or useless. Today, when we call a person or an idea "silly," we put down that person or idea.

In a similar way, the word "amusing" was once used very differently from the way it is used today. If we say that a book or movie is "amusing," we probably mean that it is funny or entertaining. The word sounds like a compliment. Yet there was a time when "amusing" people more commonly meant distracting their attention so that they could be deceived or tricked. A pickpocket, for example, might "amuse" a person while his partner stole the victim's wallet.

Another word that has changed considerably is "awesome." Many people use it today to describe something that is so great that it overwhelms us. We admire things that are awesome today,

although our admiration may also contain a little bit of wonder and even disbelief or fear. This last sense was once the main meaning of the word. People called something "awesome" if it filled them with fear and terror. An erupting volcano, for example, was considered "awesome" back then. But a day off from school was not considered "awesome"!

1. This passage is mainly about words that _____ .

● have had their meanings changed
(B) are no longer used
(C) hurt people's feelings
(D) are difficult to explain

2. This passage was written mainly to _____ .

(A) praise
● inform
(C) warn
(D) persuade

3. A person who was called "silly" long ago probably had a lot of _____ .

(A) jobs
(B) courage
● money
(D) friends

4. Long ago, the words "silly" and "amusing" both _____ .

● had meanings different from their meanings today
(B) meant almost exactly the same thing
(C) described the work a person did
(D) were taken as insults

5. The word *disbelief* in the passage means _____ .

(A) a strong opinion about something
● a feeling that something is not true
(C) an idea that something is sure to happen
(D) an idea accepted as truth

6. Which of these would have been called "amusing" long ago?

● a dishonest storekeeper
(B) a funny story
(C) a powerful volcano
(D) a rich man

7. The author of this passage probably _____ .

(A) likes to insult people
(B) speaks more than one language
● studies words
(D) lived long ago

8. Many of the words in this article are in quotation marks because _____ .

(A) they are titles
● they are being explained
(C) someone is saying them
(D) they are difficult to understand

UNIT 1

Name _____

Think of another word that is used differently today from the way it was used in the past (for example, "cool," "neat," or "bad"). Explain how the word's meaning has changed.

_____
_____
_____
_____
_____
_____
_____
_____
_____
_____
_____
_____
_____
_____
_____
_____
_____

🛑 5

Getting the Message

How does *Bulletin Board* work?

Carrie went to the school's computer room to use the new *Bulletin Board* program, which allows students from several schools to communicate by computer. At first the screen on her computer displayed a menu, a list of the different programs she could choose from. To select the *Bulletin Board* program, Carrie moved the blinking square, called the *cursor*, to the words *Bulletin Board*. Then she pressed the key that said "Enter." In a matter of seconds, the menu disappeared, and the screen said:

> Welcome to *Bulletin Board*.
> What is your name? >

Carrie typed in her name and pressed the "Enter" key again. The screen said:

> Welcome to *Bulletin Board*.
> What is your name? >Carrie Jefferson
> What is the name of your school? >

Carrie typed in the name of her school, then pressed "Enter" again, and the screen said:

➡ 7

> Welcome to *Bulletin Board*.
> What is your name? >Carrie Jefferson
> What is the name of your school? >Westerville
> What is your password? >

Carrie typed "Friday" and then pressed the "Enter" key, but the word "Friday" did not appear on the screen, where other people could see it. Only Carrie and the computer knew the password she had chosen the day she joined the *Bulletin Board* group. Each student's password was kept secret. A student who did not have a password the computer would recognize could not get into the *Bulletin Board* program.

Now the screen showed a menu that said:

> What would you like to do, Carrie Jefferson?
> S = Send a message
> Rn = Read new messages
> Ra = Read all messages
> E = Exit from *Bulletin Board*

Carrie typed "Rn" and then pressed "Enter." In a moment the screen said:

> To: Everyone
> I had a great vacation. How about the rest of you Bozos?
>   Red
>
> To: Red
> Who are you calling Bozo, you Bozo? I'm no clown! I'm taking eighth-grade math even though I'm only in sixth grade. By the way, has anyone in Mr. Wallace's class at Southside Middle School finished problem number four on tonight's homework? What answer did you get?
>   Joe Einstein

8   ➡

> To: Joe Einstein
> You are a Bozo! Who cares if you skipped a grade in math? Math isn't everything. Why don't you get a life! And if you're so smart, do problem number four yourself.
>   Chrissy
>
> To: Everyone
> There will be a city wide clothing drive next Saturday. Students from Westerville, Southside, and Central are all asked to help out. Meet in the school cafeteria at 9:00 a.m. Bring clothing that you no longer need. Be sure it is clean and in good repair.
>   LAST NEW MESSAGE
>   TO EXIT, TYPE "M" FOR MENU

Carrie typed "M" and pressed "Enter." Then she typed "S." A moment later the screen said:

> Whom do you want to address? >
> What is your message? >

Carrie typed "Everyone," and her message and then pressed "Enter." The screen said:

> To: Everyone
> Please use the *Bulletin Board* properly, or the teachers may take it off the system. My class was warned about calling each other names and sharing answers to homework problems. I'm sure the rest of you have heard the rules, too. Also, who left the message about the clothing drive? You forgot to say *which* school cafeteria to meet in.
>   Carrie of Westerville

➡ 9

Harcourt Brace School Publishers ● Unit Holistic Reading Assessment

UNIT 1

9. This passage is mainly about _____ .

   Ⓐ Carrie's day at school
   Ⓑ a computerized message system
   Ⓒ how to use a computer
   Ⓓ an argument among some computer users

10. The <u>password</u> each student has is a kind of a _____ .

   Ⓐ message from a teacher
   Ⓑ signature to put at the end of a message
   Ⓒ secret code to enter the program
   Ⓓ special word that tells about that person

11. What should Carrie type if she wants to read all of the messages students have left?

   Ⓐ Ra
   Ⓑ Rn
   Ⓒ S
   Ⓓ E

12. Which term best describes Joe Einstein?

   Ⓐ polite
   Ⓑ show-off
   Ⓒ brilliant
   Ⓓ hardworking

13. The tone of the message Red left is _____ .

   Ⓐ mysterious
   Ⓑ scary
   Ⓒ rude
   Ⓓ serious

14. Chrissy appears to dislike _____ .

   Ⓐ Red
   Ⓑ Carrie
   Ⓒ Mr. Wallace
   Ⓓ Joe Einstein

15. The message that Carrie leaves is a kind of _____ .

   Ⓐ scolding
   Ⓑ story
   Ⓒ joke
   Ⓓ puzzle

16. Which of the following is a **fact** from the passage?

   Ⓐ You *are* a Bozo!
   Ⓑ I had a great vacation.
   Ⓒ Math isn't everything.
   Ⓓ Each student's password was kept secret.

10   **Go on** →   **Stop** 11

Name _____

Explain why *Bulletin Board* is a good name for the computer program described in this passage.

_____
_____
_____
_____
_____
_____
_____
_____
_____
_____
_____
_____
_____
_____
_____
_____
_____
_____

12   **Stop**

Name _____

Think about the selections you read in "Surprises." Then complete this page. Underline the word or words in the first two items.

1. Did you enjoy reading about the things that happened in the selections in this unit?
   Yes   Sometimes   No

2. Were you able to understand all the words used in these selections?
   Yes   Most of the time   No

3. Write briefly about one thing that made reading these selections hard or one thing that made reading them easy.

_____
_____
_____

4. Which selection had the most new information? Write and explain why.

_____
_____
_____

5. If you could read more selections like one in this unit, which one would you choose? Write and tell why.

_____
_____
_____

6. Which of the selections in this unit do you think you will remember? Explain why.

_____
_____
_____

Stop 13

Harcourt Brace School Publishers ● Unit Holistic Reading Assessment

17

UNIT 2

Trophy "Case"

Directions: Read each story and the questions that follow. Fill in the answer circle in front of the correct answer for each question.

Is Uncle Hector telling the truth?

Uncle Hector was really proud that he had been a tri-state champion in the high jump when he was a seventh grader. When his nephews, Lucas and Juan, went out for track, Uncle Hector insisted they tell their coach that their uncle was *formerly* a champion. "Show him my team's 1972 trophy in the case," he said.

It seemed really important to Hector that he be remembered. So Juan went by the trophy case in the main hall at Adams Middle School to check on Uncle Hector's team trophy. He looked and looked, trying to read the engraved names and dates on the track trophies.

Juan couldn't find any trophies for any sport for the year 1971 or 1972. The dates on the trophy *collection* jumped from 1970 to 1973. "Uncle Hector must be mistaken," he told Lucas. "It doesn't look like the school had any good athletes at all those two years."

"He's probably living in a fantasy world," Lucas said.

The boys decided to have Uncle Hector prove his great abilities in high-jumping — not by actually jumping, of course, since he was now an old man in his thirties. Instead, they asked him to go home and get the individual trophy he claimed to have won. "Can't," Uncle Hector said glumly. "It got tossed out somehow while I was away in the Marines." The boys let that go without a comment, afraid that he might start telling his Marine stories again.

At Uncle Hector's insistence, Lucas asked his principal, Mr. Taggers, about the trophies. Mr. Taggers pointed out that before 1973, there was no Adams Middle School — that Uncle Hector had attended Harrison Junior High. "The Harrison trophy case was moved to the high-school building after 1970 while this building was being remodeled. Any trophies won during that time should be over there," he said.

Solving the mystery of Uncle Hector's missing trophy became a genuine challenge for Lucas and Juan. They found no Harrison trophies at the high school, either. The high-school track coach said he thought the junior-high trophies for 1971 and 1972 had been given to the Harrison County Historical Society Museum in 1973. "The remodeling at the other building was finished," he said, "and the junior-high kids were moved back there to start the newly renamed Adams Middle School."

At the museum, the boys were directed to an old glass storage case in the basement. It was so dusty they could hardly see into it, but there sat the Harrison Junior High trophies for 1971 and 1972. Yet there was no tri-state championship trophy for track in 1972! "Gosh!" Juan said. "Uncle Hector will be so disappointed."

"I think he knows what to expect!" Lucas grumbled.

"Did you find what you were looking for?" the white-haired museum director asked.

"No," Juan said sadly.

"Funny," the man said. "No one's asked about those trophies in all the years we've had them. Now yours was the second request to see them today. The other fellow asked to borrow one, and I let him take it."

"Was his name Hector Cruz?" Juan asked hopefully.

"Well," the man said, searching in the pocket of his sweater for a piece of paper, "seems to me that it was."

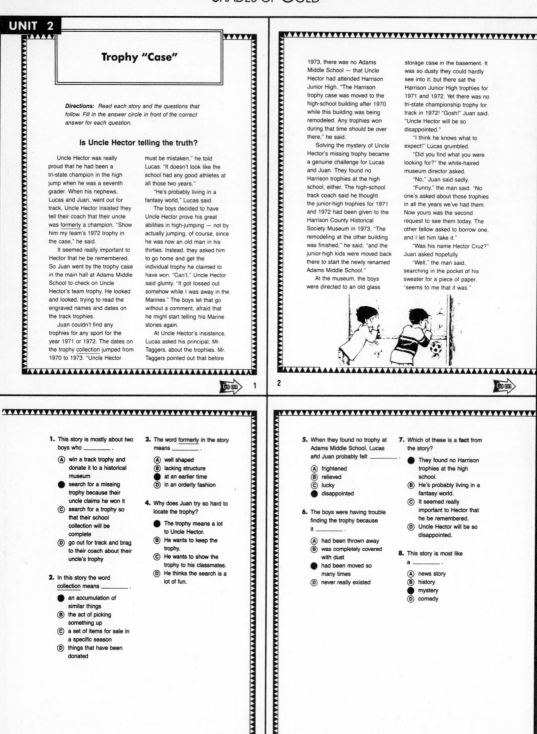

---

1. This story is mostly about two boys who _____ .

   Ⓐ win a track trophy and donate it to a historical museum

   ● search for a missing trophy because their uncle claims he won it

   Ⓒ search for a trophy so that their school collection will be complete

   Ⓓ go out for track and brag to their coach about their uncle's trophy

2. In this story the word *collection* means _____ .

   ● an accumulation of similar things

   Ⓑ the act of picking something up

   Ⓒ a set of items for sale in a specific season

   Ⓓ things that have been donated

3. The word *formerly* in the story means _____ .

   Ⓐ well shaped

   Ⓑ lacking structure

   ● at an earlier time

   Ⓓ in an orderly fashion

4. Why does Juan try so hard to locate the trophy?

   ● The trophy means a lot to Uncle Hector.

   Ⓑ He wants to keep the trophy.

   Ⓒ He wants to show the trophy to his classmates.

   Ⓓ He thinks the search is a lot of fun.

5. When they found no trophy at Adams Middle School, Lucas and Juan probably felt _____ .

   Ⓐ frightened

   Ⓑ relieved

   Ⓒ lucky

   ● disappointed

6. The boys were having trouble finding the trophy because it _____ .

   Ⓐ had been thrown away

   Ⓑ was completely covered with dust

   ● had been moved so many times

   Ⓓ never really existed

7. Which of these is a **fact** from the story?

   ● They found no Harrison trophies at the high school.

   Ⓑ He's probably living in a fantasy world.

   Ⓒ It seemed really important to Hector that he be remembered.

   Ⓓ Uncle Hector will be so disappointed.

8. This story is most like a _____ .

   Ⓐ news story

   Ⓑ history

   ● mystery

   Ⓓ comedy

Harcourt Brace School Publishers • Unit Holistic Reading Assessment

UNIT 2

Name _____

Explain why the trophy was important to Uncle Hector.

_____
_____
_____
_____
_____
_____
_____
_____
_____
_____
_____
_____
_____
_____
_____
_____
_____
_____
_____
_____

Stop 5

Go Fly a Kite!

What do you need to make a kite?

When windy weather arrives, everyone feels inclined to accept the suggestion to "go fly a kite!" If you don't happen to have a kite, it's possible to make one from materials that are likely to be found in and around your home.

What You Need

Start with a large plastic trash bag. It must be at least 24 inches long and 16 inches wide. You also need two sticks or kite dowels. Each of them should be 24 inches long and 3/16 inch wide. They can have round or square edges. If you want to use kite dowels, you can get them at a kite store, toy store, or hardware store.

You will also need the following:

• paper	• scissors	• string
• ruler	• glue	Optional:
• pen, marker, or chalk	• tape	• cloth or plastic for a tail
	• hole puncher	

6   Go on

Directions

1. Make a pattern.
First, use a large sheet of paper and a ruler to make a pattern like the one shown in Diagram 1. The pattern will be placed on the plastic trash bag, and you will trace around it to cut your kite in the right shape. Lay the trash bag on a flat surface; turn the bag so that a long edge is at the bottom. Finally, place the pattern on the bag and use a pen, marker, or chalk to trace around it on the bag.

18"   12"
8"   8"
24" (fold)
Diagram 1

2. Cut out the kite and attach sticks.
Cut around the pattern shape you traced, making sure to go through both sides of the bag. Do **not** cut along the 24-inch fold. Unfold the trash bag, and you will see that you have a whole kite. Glue the dowels to the kite as shown in Diagram 2. Let the glue dry, and then tape the dowels in place to make sure the sticks won't fall off.

Diagram 2

3. Make and attach the bridle.
The long kite-flying string must be attached to a bridle, or rigging. To make the bridle, cut a piece of string 6 feet long. Put tape on the two points of the flaps to reinforce them so they won't tear. Using scissors or a hole puncher, punch a hole through each of the two taped points. Tie one end of the bridle string through one hole, and tie the other end through the other hole. Look at Diagram 3 if you are not sure how to do this.

Diagram 3

Go on 7

---

4. Attach a kite-flying string.
You will need to fasten a kite-flying string to the center of the bridle; be sure to use a very long string so that your kite can fly high. To find the center of the bridle, bring the kite flaps exactly together. Keeping the flaps together, pull up the bridle. Use a pen to make a mark on the string right in the center. Attach the string to the center of the bridle as shown in Diagram 4. Tie it with a very tight knot.

Diagram 4

5. Make a tail.
It's possible to fly your kite without a tail, but if there is a very strong wind, a tail will help keep the kite upright and well balanced. A tail can be made from a thin 4-foot strip cut from cloth or a plastic trash bag. Use 3-inch lengths of string to tie knots every 6 inches along the strip; this will give the tail weight and will help balance the kite. The tail can be attached with safety pins, tape, or staples or by sewing. It should be centered at the bottom of the kite.

8   Go on

UNIT 2

9. This passage mostly gives information about how to _____ .
   - Ⓐ decorate a kite
   - Ⓑ make a kite pattern
   - ● make a kite of your own
   - Ⓓ attach a tail to a kite

10. In the directions a bridle is _____ .
    - ● a string connected to two sides of a kite
    - Ⓑ part of a horse's rein or harness
    - Ⓒ a wedding bouquet
    - Ⓓ a cross stick on a kite

11. Kite dowels are _____ .
    - Ⓐ tails
    - ● sticks
    - Ⓒ strings
    - Ⓓ bridles

12. The kite-flying string has to be tied to the _____ .
    - ● bridle
    - Ⓑ kite dowels
    - Ⓒ tail
    - Ⓓ pattern

13. The word reinforce in the passage means _____ .
    - Ⓐ draw attention to
    - ● strengthen
    - Ⓒ resist again
    - Ⓓ encourage

14. The kite is probably made from a plastic trash bag rather than cardboard because the _____ .
    - Ⓐ cardboard is harder to cut
    - Ⓑ cardboard won't bend easily
    - ● trash bag weighs less
    - Ⓓ trash bag is less likely to tear

15. The information in this passage is mostly presented as a _____ .
    - Ⓐ list of reasons
    - Ⓑ story
    - Ⓒ comparison of ideas
    - ● sequence of steps

16. In which book is this passage most likely to be found?
    - ● Do-It-Yourself Projects
    - Ⓑ An Expert's Guide to Aircraft
    - Ⓒ Poems About Kites, Birds, and Butterflies
    - Ⓓ The History of Flight

9

10

Name _____

Suppose you didn't have a plastic trash bag to use in making your kite. What could you use in place of a plastic trash bag? Explain why you think so.

_____
_____
_____
_____
_____
_____
_____
_____
_____
_____
_____
_____
_____
_____
_____

11

Name _____

Think about the selections you read in "Heroes." Then complete this page. Underline the word or words in the first two items.

1. As you read these selections, could you see in your mind what was happening?
   Yes   Sometimes   No

2. How well did these selections hold your attention?
   Very well   Fairly well   Not well

3. Write a brief explanation and tell why some selections did or did not hold your attention.
   _____
   _____
   _____

4. List some ways you think you could become a better reader.
   _____
   _____
   _____

5. Which character in a selection in this unit did you particularly like or dislike? Tell why.
   _____
   _____
   _____

6. Which of the selections in this unit do you think would make the best movie? Tell why.
   _____
   _____
   _____

13

Harcourt Brace School Publishers ● Unit Holistic Reading Assessment

UNIT 3

Kendall Goes Free
by Dann Denny

Directions: Read each story and the questions that follow. Fill in the answer circle in front of the correct answer for each question.

How does Alison feel about giving up her pet?

This summer, on her 7th birthday, our first-born daughter received the most thrilling gift of her life — a box turtle.

Alison's face lit up like a sunrise when this sluggish, dome-backed reptile was placed into her hands. She named him Kendall, and talked to him as a mother would a child.

"Oh Kendall," she would say, holding him to her face and pressing her nose against his. "You're such a sweetheart."

Compared to most reptiles, Kendall enjoyed a regal lifestyle. I built for him a lavish villa. It was a 4- by 6-foot wooden box — complete with swimming pool, sandy beach area, and shoebox bed. He dined on hotdogs and sliced turkey.

If Kendall was not luxuriating in his home, he was with Alison. When she lay on the couch and watched TV, she would place Kendall on her chest and gently stroke the back of his neck with her finger. When she swooped back and forth on her tree swing, Kendall would ride in her lap.

Eventually, she coaxed Kendall to snatch pieces of hotdog from her hand. With the meat in his mouth, he often would burrow beneath a blanket or bed pillow, concealing all but his stubby tail.

"Silly Kendall," she would say with a giggle. "You're not very good at playing hide and seek."

But all was not bliss. In the late evening, my wife and I could hear Kendall's claws scratching against the walls of his home. He would pull himself upright, then topple over onto his back with a loud *thud*. Undeterred, he would try — again and again — to scale his way to freedom.

As we listened, we realized Kendall would have to go. The question was when. Fortunately, Kendall gave us the answer. He stopped eating.

"Daddy, you have to call a veterinarian right away," said Alison when she noticed the chunks of uneaten meat in Kendall's home. "He's sick."

"He's not sick," I told her. "Kendall wants to be free. He loves you, but he wants to be free."

The next day, in the early evening, Alison and I went to a small creek that winds its way lazily through some woodlands behind a neighborhood park. The air was heavy, and the first shadows of dusk were beginning to slant across the water.

Cradling Kendall in her hands, Alison tiptoed through some inch-deep water onto an island of smooth rocks. She lifted him to her face and kissed him on the nose.

"Goodbye, sweetheart. I love you."

Forcing a tight-lipped smile, she gently laid him in the shallow stream. As her fingers pulled away, Kendall lay motionless in the water, his legs dangling limply by his sides as the current carried him slowly downstream.

Suddenly, his neck shot up like a periscope. As his eyes scanned his boundless surroundings and his pinhead-sized nostrils smelled the rich aroma of freedom, Kendall's webbed feet began to paddle.

Alison's face grew taut as she watched him churn toward the opposite side of the stream.

"Goodbye, Kendall. I love you," she called out. "I'll never forget you. Never ever."

Kendall climbed out of the water, clambered up a muddy bank and disappeared into a patch of tall grass.

I glanced at Alison's face. She was staring vacantly at the bank, her eyes locked on the grassy area where Kendall had vanished from sight.

1

2

"Are you sure he'll be all right, Daddy?" she asked.

"Yes, he'll be fine."

"And happy?"

"Very."

She shrugged her shoulders and heaved a big sigh. Then, after several moments of silence, her face brightened.

"Hey, I've got a great idea," she said, a trace of excitement returning to her voice. "Let's collect some of these shiny rocks."

3

---

1. The person who is telling this story is _____ .
   - (A) Alison
   - (B) Alison's father
   - (C) Alison's mother
   - (D) a reporter

2. In this story the word scale means _____ .
   - (A) climb
   - (B) clean
   - (C) a turtle's skin
   - (D) machine used to weigh something

3. The word luxuriating in this story means _____ .
   - (A) spending a lot of money
   - (B) growing bigger and bigger
   - (C) enjoying a good life
   - (D) staying very healthy

4. What caused Alison to think that Kendall was sick?
   - (A) He lay motionless in the water.
   - (B) He stopped eating.
   - (C) He hid under a blanket.
   - (D) He ate from her hand.

4

UNIT 3

5. Alison and her father put Kendall into the stream because they _____.

   Ⓐ no longer wanted to take care of him
   Ⓑ wanted to see if he could swim
   Ⓒ wanted him to clean himself
   Ⓓ thought that was best for him

6. What finally became of Kendall?

   Ⓐ He returned to Alison's yard.
   Ⓑ He drowned in the stream.
   Ⓒ He became a free turtle.
   Ⓓ He got lost in the tall grass.

7. At the end of the story, Alison seems to believe that _____.

   Ⓐ a free life will be best for Kendall
   Ⓑ her father made the wrong decision about Kendall
   Ⓒ Kendall needs some real rocks in his box at home
   Ⓓ she can come and see Kendall when she wants

8. What lesson does the author of this story probably want to teach us?

   Ⓐ Hotdogs aren't good for turtles to eat.
   Ⓑ Wild animals should not be kept as pets.
   Ⓒ Children should obey their parents.
   Ⓓ Children should be taught how to name their pets.

(Stop) 5

Name _____

Tell what Kendall was probably thinking when he stopped eating.

_____

_____

_____

_____

_____

_____

_____

_____

_____

_____

_____

_____

_____

_____

_____

_____

_____

_____

_____

_____

_____

_____

_____

6 *(Stop)*

The Hump

What was life like for these pilots?

During the war between the United States and Japan, pilots in the U.S. Army Air Corps flew supplies from India into China using C-47s and C-46s, two-engine transport planes. The Himalayas, parallel chains of mountains between India and China, include some of the tallest peaks in the world and were known to these men as "The Hump."

Years after the war was over, the Air Force mailed the diary of one of these pilots to his family. From it they learned more about the mission, the camp where the men lived, and one way that the men passed their free time.

OCT. 24, 1943

The Hump is wild, beautiful, and majestic. It is certainly the most difficult territory in the world. Many of the peaks we fly over reach up to 17,000 and 18,000 feet above sea level. At night, we take a direct route into China, right over two Japanese airfields. We are unarmed and unescorted by our fighter planes, and we carry gasoline as cargo. Too frequently, our planes, especially C-46s, are shot down or crash into the mountains.

This is tropical country, and our runways are set right in a jungle of brush. The airfield is in a valley between two of the mountain ranges. Anti-aircraft guns poke their mean-looking snouts up from various posts.

War is a serious business here; this field has suffered bomb raids. Japanese outposts and fields are only fifty miles away. Deep slit-trenches are provided for us to dive into during air raids. We wear our army automatic pistols and keep our gas masks and helmets close by at all times.

During a recent bombing alert, I stayed in the mess tent long enough to eat several desserts left behind by my buddies who quickly took cover. Enlisted men eat their meals outdoors out of mess kits. We officers eat inside on plates. The food is not so hot. Tonight "C rations" were served. I think they must taste like dog food.

(Go on →) 7

We are assigned to a small tent with no flooring, and we sleep on army canvas cots — no sheets and no pillows or mattresses; just two blankets. By morning, I nearly freeze. The other day, I cut down some bamboo and made a clothes-rail, and a rack for our baggage. We have an outside latrine, located by a big banana tree.

OCT. 25, 1943

We have a regular menagerie here. Immediately back of our tents are two monkeys. About fifty yards down the way, one of the boys has a tame leopard. He raised it from a cub. I was playing with it today, but it plays too rough.

We visited a private about a mile from here whose hobby is catching and raising snakes found in this region. He has several pythons, one of them eleven feet in length. Running around loose on the floor were two lizards some eighteen inches long.

When we entered, the private was busily engaged in trying to induce one of some ten-odd snakes in one cage to eat a white mouse. The mouse either had a charmed life, or the reptiles weren't hungry. Several snakes got into a fight, and the private had to open their mouths and pry them loose. One snake in this cage was a tree snake, whose chief claim to fame is his ability to flatten his body and glide through the air from one tree to another.

In another cage were four or five species of deadly poisonous vipers. In still another, there were six cobras. Reaching into this cage, the private pulled out a large snake and pried its mouth open. Pushing gently on one of its extended fangs, he caused several drops of deadly venom to ooze out onto his fingernail. Assuring me that the snake rarely struck and that he had been bitten only twenty-one times since he started collecting snakes, he placed the snake in my hands. I was a bit skeptical, especially so when it spread its hood and, with forked tongue darting energetically in and out, began weaving its head about six inches in front of my face.

The private explained how he gets most of the venom out of his body when he is bitten. He handles all of his snakes freely and without fear, claiming that any snake could become accustomed to handling in several hours. Maybe so.

(Go on →) 8

Harcourt Brace School Publishers ● Unit Holistic Reading Assessment

9. The October 24 and 25 entries in this diary are mostly about a transport pilot's _____ .

Ⓐ description of flying battles he experienced during a war
Ⓑ account of Japanese air strength at the beginning of a war
Ⓒ mission and camp life during a war
Ⓓ memories of his buddies after a war

10. The introduction to the passage tells us all of the following information **except** _____ .

Ⓐ where the pilot flew
Ⓑ the name of the pilot
Ⓒ the pilots' nickname for the mountains
Ⓓ the type of plane the pilot flew

11. The word <u>unarmed</u> in this passage means _____ .

Ⓐ ready for battle
Ⓑ not threatened
Ⓒ missing some limbs
Ⓓ without weapons

12. The diary suggests that the Himalayas are _____ .

Ⓐ ugly and frightening
Ⓑ wild but beautiful
Ⓒ tame and boring
Ⓓ low but dangerous

13. As it is described here, life in the tents seems _____ .

Ⓐ relaxing
Ⓑ luxurious
Ⓒ uncomfortable
Ⓓ unexciting

14. Which sentence best summarizes how the pilot probably felt about life in the camp?

Ⓐ He did not enjoy it but tried to make the best of it.
Ⓑ He thought of it as a really worthwhile experience.
Ⓒ He disliked it, so he gave up trying.
Ⓓ He was lonely and wanted to go home.

15. The word <u>skeptical</u> in this passage means _____ .

Ⓐ angry
Ⓑ doubting
Ⓒ amused
Ⓓ trusting

16. If you were to fly over the Himalayas today, you would be most certain to see _____ .

Ⓐ high mountains
Ⓑ tame leopards
Ⓒ vipers in cages
Ⓓ transport airplanes

9 10

Name _____

Use information from the passage to explain how the author feels about war.

_____
_____
_____
_____
_____
_____
_____
_____
_____
_____
_____
_____
_____

11

Name _____

Think about the selections you read in "A World Away." Then complete this page. Underline the word or words in the first two items.

1. Would you look for selections like these to read on your own?
Yes   Maybe   No

2. Were you able to understand the vocabulary in these selections?
Yes   Most of the time   No

3. Write about the most interesting thing you learned in this unit.
_____
_____

4. Do you read more or less now than you have in the past? Write and tell what would make you read more.
_____
_____

5. Choose the selection you liked most or least in this unit. Write your feelings about it.
_____
_____

6. In which of the places described in the unit's selections would you choose to live? Explain your choices.
_____
_____
_____

13

UNIT 4

The Dragon That Munched
by Suzanne Burgoyne Dieckman

Directions: Read each story and the questions that follow. Fill in the answer circle in front of the correct answer for each question.

What was unusual about Roger's experimental computer?

"Ro-ger," his mother called up the stairs, "have you finished your homework?"

"I wish," said Roger to Dragon, "there was no such word as homework."

Actually, Roger didn't say that. He typed it on Dragon's keyboard. Dragon was a computer. A new, hush-hush, experimental model computer that Roger's dad (a very important scientist) was working on. Roger wasn't supposed to be playing with Dragon, of course. But his friend Charlie was a computer whiz, so Roger needed to practice to keep up.

The prompt **Do next?** appeared in green letters on Dragon's monitor.

Roger was getting a headache from concentrating so hard. Also, he was hungry.

Eat, he typed.

Eat what? replied Dragon.

Cookie, typed Roger.

Yum, printed Dragon. **Thank you.**

Roger turned off Dragon and went downstairs to the kitchen.

"Mom," he said, "may I have a nibblefritz?"

"What?" said his mother.

"I said, I'd like a chompsickle."

"What?"

No matter how hard Roger tried, he couldn't say the word *cookie*. Finally, he drew a picture.

Roger went back upstairs to Dragon.

Dragon, he typed, **did you eat the word** — Roger discovered he couldn't type *cookie*, either — **nummiewat?**

Yum, printed Dragon. **Eat next?**

Roger thought for a moment. Slowly, he typed into the computer, **homework.**

"Roger," his mother called up the stairs, "have you finished your thinkdoodle?"

"I'm doing it now, Mom," he yelled. He went to the phone and called his friend Charlie.

"Hey, Charlie, what are you doing?"

"I'm doing my memorpickle."

"That's what I thought," said Roger. "It can wait. Come over here. I've got something to show you."

Since Charlie lived next door, it wasn't long before he was standing next to Roger, blinking at Dragon's screen. "A computer that eats words? And after Dragon eats a word, nobody can say it? Hmm," he muttered. "What are you going to do?"

"Well," said Roger, "I was thinking of all the words I could feed to Dragon. Words I'd like to get rid of. Like *karate lessons*. I mean, my parents couldn't make me go, could they, if they couldn't say it?"

"I see what you mean," Charlie said. "But your vision is limited. Think big."

Before Roger could stop him, Charlie leaned over and typed **nuclear missile** after Dragon's **Eat next?** prompt.

Roger shook his head. He hurried to wash the dishes so he could watch the evening news.

"And the crisis of the hour," the newscaster was saying, "is the breakdown in the arms negotiation talks. At the special session tonight, negotiators on both sides found themselves unable to pronounce the words *bumbledy boomdoom*."

Roger ran for the phone. "Charlie," he whispered, "get over here. Fast. We're in trouble."

Roger waited for Charlie to arrive before switching on Dragon.

"What do we do?" Roger demanded. "We've got to get him to give the words back."

Suddenly Roger sat down at the keyboard and began typing.

"What are you doing?" Charlie asked.

Chocolate fudge cake, typed Roger frantically. **Pistachio ice cream. Licorice sticks.**

Yum, printed Dragon. **Yum. Yum.**

Banana split. Coconut doughnut. Pizza with anchovies...

Yum, printed Dragon. **Yum.** All at once his letters flickered, like a hiccough. **Yuk.**

Dragon's monitor suddenly filled with words, spewing across the screen faster than Roger could read them. Roger took a deep breath and crossed his fingers. "Cookie," he said.

"How did you do that?" Charlie blinked in amazement.

Roger shrugged. "I just remembered what happened to *me* one time when I ate a lot of that stuff."

"You made Dragon upchuck all the words? By feeding him all that stuff?" Charlie blinked in disgust. "Yuk."

---

1. Dragon is _____ .

   ● Roger's nickname
   B) Roger's father's computer
   C) a new computer game
   D) the name of Roger's friend

2. Why was Roger using his dad's experimental computer?

   A) He wanted to learn how computers work.
   B) He had to do his homework.
   ● He wanted to keep up with his friend.
   D) He wanted to get a better grade in school.

3. In this story the word *monitor* means _____ .

   A) watch closely
   ● a computer screen
   C) follow directions
   D) a student helper

4. Roger's friend is _____ .

   ● very knowledgeable about computers
   B) the first one to finish the homework
   C) too busy to help him with his problem
   D) the one who got Roger into trouble

Harcourt Brace School Publishers ● Unit Holistic Reading Assessment

Harcourt Brace School Publishers ● Unit Holistic Reading Assessment

UNIT 4

5. The computer "ate" words whenever Roger or Charlie _____ .

Ⓐ said the words aloud
Ⓑ used nonsense words
Ⓒ turned it on
● typed the words on the keyboard

6. Roger first realized what the computer was doing when _____ .

Ⓐ he couldn't say the word *cookie*
Ⓑ his mother asked him if he had finished his homework
Ⓒ the word *cookie* came up on the monitor
Ⓓ his friend told him

7. When Roger watched the news, he realized that _____ .

Ⓐ he had forgotten to finish his homework
Ⓑ he had missed his karate lessons
Ⓒ the computer made it impossible to use certain words
Ⓓ Charlie had played a trick on him

8. Roger figured out how to solve the problem by _____ .

Ⓐ reading the instruction manual
Ⓑ remembering something that had happened to him
Ⓒ finding out about a similar problem on the TV news
Ⓓ asking his father for advice

Name _____

Suppose you had a computer like Roger's. Write a paragraph telling how you would use your computer and what you would make it do.

_____
_____
_____
_____
_____
_____
_____
_____
_____
_____
_____
_____
_____
_____
_____
_____
_____
_____
_____
_____
_____
_____

Stop 5

6 Stop

Julie's Special Job
by Ed and Ruth Radlauer

Why is Dad doing all the work?

[*Julie Brand has persuaded her parents to let her raise a golden retriever puppy that will later be trained as a guide dog for a blind person. Julie is to keep Goblin, the dog, for 15 months before turning her over to an organization named Guide Dogs of the Desert, which will train her.*]

One Sunday morning, Julie slept until 9 o'clock. When she got up and looked out the window, Dad had moved the doghouse onto the grass where he was hosing it out. The old blankets from inside the pup's house were hanging on the clothesline.

Dressing quickly, she ran out to the yard. "What are you doing, Dad?" she asked.

"Just all the stuff you promised to do." He sounded angry.

"Nobody said you had to clean house for a dog."

"How would you like to sleep in the same sheets for several weeks?"

It hardly seemed that important. "Come on, Goblin." She stomped back into the house. In her room she hugged the golden retriever. "Oh, Goblin, I hope Dad doesn't make me send you back."

Goblin cocked her head to one side and whimpered with Julie. She burrowed her nose under Julie's hand, begging to be petted. "Besides," Julie told the pup, "you sleep in my room most of the time now anyway."

Julie began to feel better until she looked up to see Dad standing in the doorway. "I knew I'd end up doing all the work," he said.

Her shoulders sagged and she felt like crying. "But Dad, you move faster than anyone else in the house. You talk to *me* about patience—"

"What about it?"

She took a chance. "Well, you're not even <u>patient</u> enough to let other people do things at their own speed."

He started to answer, but kept quiet.

"Besides," she went on. "I think you *like* to do all the grooming and feeding. You never give *me* a chance to."

Dad sat down on the floor and rested his elbows on his knees. "You know, I think you're right."

"You do six things while the rest of us are thinking about one."

Dad's mad look went away. "I never got to have a dog when I was a kid. You know what Goblin did yesterday? She fetched the newspaper for me. How about that?"

"Dad, I *like* to <u>groom</u> and feed Goblin. She's calm and lovable when I groom her and not so jumpy and frustrating. And if you feed her all the time, she's going to love you more than she does

me, and *I'm* supposed to be the puppy raiser."

"Hmmm. I guess you're trying to tell me to mind my own business and let you do your job, huh?" Dad stood up and gazed around the room. Looking disappointed, he dusted the edge of a bookshelf and pushed the books into an even row.

Julie smiled at him. "I don't mind if you groom or feed once in awhile."

"Okay," Dad said. "Just let me know when it's my turn — maybe when you have too much to do."

"Dad?"

"Yes?"

"You love Goblin, too, don't you?"

He looked embarrassed. "Sure do," he admitted. "She's some dog!"

Go on 7

8 Go on

25

SHADES OF GOLD

UNIT 4

9. This story is mainly about _____ .
- Ⓐ how to raise a dog
- Ⓑ a dog that gets into trouble
- ● a girl and her father discussing their feelings
- Ⓓ a girl who forgets to clean her room

10. In this story the word groom means _____ .
- Ⓐ someone who takes care of horses
- ● to brush and clean a dog's hair
- Ⓒ a man who is getting married
- Ⓓ to help someone get ready

11. In this story the word patient means _____ .
- Ⓐ curious
- ● willing to wait
- Ⓒ stubborn
- Ⓓ polite

12. Why does Dad act angry?
- Ⓐ He thinks Julie is hiding from him.
- Ⓑ He thinks the dog does not like him.
- ● He is having to do Julie's work.
- Ⓓ He does not like having a dog around.

13. How does Dad really feel about doing things for Goblin?
- ● He likes caring for her.
- Ⓑ He is too tired to care for her.
- Ⓒ He is upset about getting dirty.
- Ⓓ He feels tricked into all the work.

14. When she goes back to her room, Julie is worried that _____ .
- Ⓐ she has made Goblin sick
- Ⓑ the dog does not like her
- Ⓒ Dad might get rid of Goblin
- Ⓓ her room does not look tidy

15. Which sentence shows that Dad never gives Julie a chance to do her own work?
- Ⓐ Goblin cocked her head to one side and whimpered.
- Ⓑ Dad was cleaning the doghouse before Julie got up.
- Ⓒ Julie's shoulders sagged and she felt like crying.
- Ⓓ Dad never had a dog when he was young.

16. Which of these is a fact from the story?
- Ⓐ One Sunday morning Julie slept until 9 o'clock.
- Ⓑ I like to groom and feed Goblin.
- Ⓒ It hardly seemed that important.
- Ⓓ I hope Dad doesn't make me send you back.

9

10

Name _____

How does Dad feel about Goblin? Explain your reasons.

11

Name _____

Think about the selections you read in "Light Moments." Then complete this page. Underline the word or words in the first two items.

1. Did the selections remind you of things you have read before?
   Yes   I'm not sure   No

2. Would you choose these selections to read on your own?
   Yes   Maybe   No

3. Choose one selection that you might advise a friend to read. Write and explain why.

4. If you had a personal library, what kinds of literature would you include in it? List your choices.

5. List one or two things that made the selections in this unit easy or hard to enjoy and explain why.

6. Do these selections have enough action for you? Write a brief explanation of why or why not.

13

Harcourt Brace School Publishers ● Unit Holistic Reading Assessment

26

UNIT 5

Nedu

Directions: Read each story and the questions that follow. Fill in the answer circle in front of the correct answer for each question.

How did Nedu escape drowning?

Nedu was still very young the winter that he asked his father if he could join the village fishermen in fishing for the yellow mullet, a small fish that travels in enormous groups. Nedu's people, the Imragen, were members of a small tribe who live in Mauritania, just north of the equator in western Africa. The Imragen have lived on the seashore for centuries, fishing with nets made from the fibers of desert plants. Over the years, they have learned that if they beat the waters with a board, dolphins will drive schools of fish into the shallow water where the Imragen can catch them in their nets.

Each winter, if it is a good season, many schools of fish move south, and the dolphins are there to drive them to shore. If the dolphins do not come, the fish pass by too far out to sea for the fishermen to catch them. The dolphins ensure the survival of the Imragen.

Nedu was an excellent swimmer, and he had often swum out far enough to find himself among a group of dolphins. He swam alongside them, sometimes holding onto the dorsal fin on a dolphin's back. The dolphins were his friends.

When Nedu asked his father about taking part in the winter fishing, his father just looked down at him. Nedu was young and wouldn't be much help to the fishermen, but his desire was clear. Father put his hand on the boy's shoulder and reminded him that he must not get in the way.

1

Very early in the morning, the men huddled down among the dunes to escape the harsh sea wind. Standing like a statue, staring out at the sea and shading his eyes with his hand, Nedu seemed unaware of the cold. Soon, far out at sea, he saw a slight color change in the water. The yellow mullet were migrating south. A man rushed out to slap the water's surface with a board. Before long the dorsal fins of dolphins cut through the waves as they came toward the shore, driving the fish before them.

The men raised long poles draped with heavy nets to their shoulders. The nets were soon filled with thousands of fish, flinging themselves into the air and swimming at high speeds. The water boiled with leaping fish and dolphins swimming around the nets.

Nedu was so filled with awe that he had been unable to move. Suddenly he felt himself being pulled into the water as his foot became entangled, or caught, in one of the nets. Salty water rushed into his mouth. Almost at the same time, he felt the powerful body of a dolphin under his own. The force of the dolphin's movement freed his foot. Instinctively, as his body rolled over, he grabbed the dorsal fin on the dolphin's back and was pulled toward shore. As the water became shallow, the dolphin turned and swam out to sea, and Nedu stumbled onto the beach. For the rest of the morning, he watched the skillful fishermen as they dragged the heavy nets to the beach. Nedu was lost in his thoughts about the wonders of the partnership between his people and the dolphins. His own experience made him grateful to be part of it.

2

1. This story is mainly about _____ .
   - (A) how dolphins survive in the sea
   - ● a beneficial partnership between a boy and a dolphin
   - (C) the relationship between a boy and his father
   - (D) how to use nets to catch schools of fish

2. The word mullet in the story refers to a type of _____ .
   - (A) fiber
   - (B) net
   - (C) dolphin
   - ● fish

3. The word entangled in the story means _____ .
   - ● caught
   - (B) involved
   - (C) arranged
   - (D) dragged

4. The word Imragen in the story refers to _____ .
   - (A) Nedu's father's name
   - (B) a seashore in western Africa
   - ● a tribe in Mauritania
   - (D) the season for fishing

3

5. One fisherman slapped the water with a board because it _____ .
   - (A) scared the dolphins away so the men could catch the fish
   - ● made the dolphins drive the mullet toward the shore
   - (C) stunned the fish into staying still
   - (D) signaled to the fishermen to be ready with the nets

6. Far out at sea, Nedu saw a color change in the water because the _____ .
   - (A) wind was blowing the water
   - (B) man was beating the water with a board
   - ● yellow mullet were swimming in huge groups
   - (D) sun was reflecting in the water

7. It is most likely that the dolphin that helped Nedu _____ .
   - (A) was lost
   - (B) didn't hear the sound of the board on the water
   - (C) was trying to tear the nets
   - ● recognized him as a friend who had swum with him

8. Which lesson can best be learned from this story?
   - ● Men and animals can often work together.
   - (B) If you want a job done right, do it yourself.
   - (C) Young people should always listen to their elders.
   - (D) It is impossible to control the forces of nature.

4

SHADES OF GOLD

UNIT 5

Name _____

Explain why the dolphins are so important to the Imragen.

_____
_____
_____
_____
_____
_____
_____
_____
_____
_____
_____
_____
_____
_____
_____
_____
_____

Stop 5

Oceans

How much water is found on earth?

Water was once thought to be one of the four basic elements (Earth-Air-Fire-Water). Water covers approximately 70 percent of the earth's surface, or 139,434,000 square miles (388,755,999 square kilometers), while the land surface of the earth is only 57,506,000 square miles (148,940,540 square kilometers). There is just about the same amount of water on earth today as there was thousands of years ago.

Without water, our planet would be uninhabitable, or unfit to live in, because human beings, animals, and plants depend on water for life. It has been estimated that as many as nine out of ten organisms in the world live in the oceans.

While water covers 70 percent of the earth's surface, less than one percent is fresh water that we can drink. More than three-quarters of the fresh water along the earth's surface is frozen in the Antarctic ice cap.

The table on the next page provides some interesting statistics regarding the area and volume of water that is present on earth. Use the table to help answer the questions that follow this passage.

Go On 7

THE VITAL STATISTICS OF WATER

	Area* (square miles)	Volume* (cubic miles)	% of Total*
SALT WATER			
The oceans	139,500,000	317,000,000	97.2
Inland seas & saline (saltwater) lakes	270,000	25,000	0.008
FRESH WATER			
Freshwater lakes	330,000	30,000	0.009
All rivers (average level)		300	0.0001
Antarctic ice cap	6,000,000	6,300,000	1.9
Arctic ice cap & glaciers	900,000	680,000	0.15
Water in the atmosphere		3,100	0.001
GROUND WATER			
Surface		1,000,000	0.31
Deep-lying		1,000,000	0.31
TOTAL (approximate)		326,000,000	100.00

*All figures are estimated
Source: U.S. Department of the Interior

8 Go On

---

9. According to the table, underlined{saline} refers to water that is _____ .
   - (A) frozen
   - (B) fresh
   - (C) salty
   - (D) deep-lying

10. The word underlined{uninhabitable} in the passage means _____ .
   - (A) very customary
   - (B) not suitable for plant or animal life
   - (C) lived in before
   - (D) sparsely populated by living beings

11. According to the table, all rivers on the earth combined make up _____ .
   - (A) 300 cubic miles
   - (B) 97 percent of the total water
   - (C) 30,000 cubic miles
   - (D) 900,000 square miles

12. Cubic miles are used in the table to show water's _____ .
   - (A) quality
   - (B) temperature
   - (C) depth
   - (D) volume

Go On 9

Harcourt Brace School Publishers ● Unit Holistic Reading Assessment

28

Harcourt Brace School Publishers ● Unit Holistic Reading Assessment

UNIT 5

13. The total volume of water on the earth is _____ .

(A) 326,000,000 cubic miles
(B) 139,500,000 square miles
(C) 317,000,000 cubic miles
(D) 147,000,000 square miles

14. According to the passage, about ninety percent of the world's organisms live in _____ .

(A) the Arctic
(B) glaciers
(C) the oceans
(D) fresh water

15. The Antarctic ice cap has more than three-quarters of the earth's _____ .

(A) glaciers
(B) fresh water
(C) atmospheric water
(D) salt water

16. The way information is presented in this passage shows _____ .

(A) general facts and statistics on a subject
(B) causes of a particular event
(C) reasons to support a point of view
(D) the order in which things happened

10 ⬛Stop

Name _____

Based on what you read in this passage, explain why most of the earth's water cannot be used for drinking.

_____
_____
_____
_____
_____
_____
_____
_____
_____
_____
_____
_____
_____
_____
_____
_____
_____
_____
_____
_____
_____
_____
_____
_____
_____

11 ⬛Stop

Name _____

Think about the selections you read in "Oceans." Then complete this page. Underline the word or words in the first two items.

1. Did you have trouble keeping your mind on these selections?
Not often   Sometimes   Often

2. Would you like to read more selections like these?
Yes   Maybe   No

3. Write a brief explanation about why you do or do not like the type of selections in this unit.

_____
_____
_____

4. In what ways have your reading interests changed as a result of reading the selections in this unit? List some of them.

_____
_____
_____

5. Do you think you will remember these selections for a long time? Explain why or why not.

_____
_____
_____

6. Write about the most interesting thing you learned in this unit.

_____
_____
_____

13 ⬛Stop

UNIT 6

Into the Past

Directions: Read each story and the questions that follow. Fill in the answer circle in front of the correct answer for each question.

What kind of town did Tim visit?

Tim was exhausted. For three weeks he and his parents had been camping along the coast of Maine. He could hardly wait to get home and hug Chipper, his dog. He wanted to sit out on their deck and drink cold milk. Then he would watch TV before going up to sleep in his own bed.

His dad turned off the highway onto a side road, intending to stop at a clothing factory Mother wanted to visit.

"Oh, oh!" Tim's dad said, pulling the car over.

"Detour," his mom read from a sign. Tim sighed. A detour always made him feel so uncomfortable. Instead of seeming like an unexpected adventure, it always seemed foreboding somehow, like a warning.

His dad followed the detour sign down an unpaved road. For nearly a hour, they saw no cars or people. Finally they drove into a little town where people were milling around outside. "How charming!" Mother said. "They're all in costumes that look at least 150 years old!" All their houses seemed quite old and quaint, too. Some were log cabins.

The people stared in amazement at Tim and his family. As Tim's dad pulled the car over, a crowd gathered around. Yet many people stood back, some distance away. The women stared at Tim's mother, who looked a bit conspicuous in her slacks. Lots of people leaned forward, staring at the car.

NOWHERE
POPULATION 112

"Where's your horse?" someone in the crowd called out. Dad thought it was a wonderful joke and laughed out loud. Tim couldn't help noticing that there were no other cars in sight.

Two boys at the edge of the crowd started waving at him. "Patrick!" they called. "Where in tarnation have you been? We thought you went bear hunting and got lost!" Tim couldn't convince the boys that his name was not Patrick. He began answering to the name and soon became friends with the boys and felt right at home.

Tim's mother noticed some interesting stores and decided to do some shopping. What a wonderful day she had! No one would accept her money, so she bartered by trading things she had with her for things made by women in the town. Tim's dad went through the shops where candles and saddles were made and saw one where horses were shoed.

When it came time to leave, Father asked the way to Philadelphia. Everyone found this amusing, since there was only the one road in and out of the town.

"You're not going off again?" one of the boys asked Tim. The boys clung to the open windows of the car, talking to Tim inside. They recoiled very quickly, however, at the sound of the car's engine.

"So long again, Patrick," Tim heard one boy call out as Father began to drive away. Tim looked back and saw a hand-painted sign that said, "Nowhere. Population 112."

"Their act is very convincing," Tim's father said. "They even have calendars that say 1814. I'm surprised they don't attract more tourists."

"You know," Tim's mother said, "they had just finished making this jam — but the date on the jar label says 1814! Aren't they clever!"

Tim settled back for a long ride, but all at once they rounded a corner, and there was the highway right outside their hometown!

Tim yawned, wondering how it had gotten dark so fast. Inside their house, Chipper jumped up to greet him. Tim gave Chipper a hug; then he went to the desk and took out a map. He studied the map carefully for several minutes — but he could not find "Nowhere" on it anywhere.

---

1. This story is mostly about a boy and his family who _____ .

- (A) spend a wonderful day shopping with friends
- ● follow a detour that leads them back in time
- (C) see no cars or people after they take a detour
- (D) go camping along the coast of Maine

2. This story could best be described as a _____ .

- (A) scientific report
- (B) news article
- (C) comedy
- ● science fiction story

3. The word foreboding in the story means _____ .

- ● predicting bad things in advance
- (B) giving extra signs
- (C) staying without permission
- (D) waiting again

4. The word bartered in the story means _____ .

- (A) worked
- (B) left
- ● exchanged
- (D) begged

5. The words in the story that help you know what bartered means are _____ .

- (A) everyone laughed
- (B) by trading things
- (C) started waving at him
- (D) leaned forward

6. The author of this story wants readers to think that the town is _____ .

- (A) strange
- (B) modern
- (C) unfriendly
- (D) dangerous

7. The author says that "Nowhere" is not on a map in order to show that the town is _____ .

- (A) in a foreign country
- (B) a tourist attraction
- (C) not a real place
- (D) Tim's hometown

8. Which question is **not** answered in the story?

- (A) Why did the detour seem to result in a time change?
- (B) Where were Tim and his parents at the end of the story?
- (C) What was unusual about Mother's jar of jam?
- (D) Where had the family spent their vacation earlier?

Harcourt Brace School Publishers ● Unit Holistic Reading Assessment

UNIT 6

Name _____

Think about the clues the author provided in the story. Then write some of the clues the author gave to make readers think it really *was* 1814 in the town of Nowhere.

_____
_____
_____
_____
_____
_____
_____
_____
_____
_____
_____
_____
_____
_____
_____
_____
_____
_____
_____
_____

5

The Pony Express

What was the pony express, and what caused it to end?

Getting mail to the Far West was a difficult and time-consuming task in 1860. Stagecoaches took four weeks or more to make the run from Missouri to California. To speed up the mail, a pony service that included 190 stations manned with 400 keepers and helpers was initiated. The first run — made on April 14, 1860 — covered 1,966 miles over the desert and mountains from the western end of the railway at St. Joseph, Missouri, to Sacramento, California. It required ten and one-half days and forty riders.

The company that established the pony express bought 400 fast ponies and hired a team of eighty expert riders. They traveled more than ten miles an hour over mountains and up to twenty-five miles an hour on flat stretches. The riders stayed on one pony for ten to fifteen miles, then changed mounts and rode at top speed to the next relay station.

The keeper would run out with a fresh mount as the rider approached and sounded a little horn he carried with him. The rider jumped from his mount, threw his pouch on the new pony, and sped away within two minutes. The pouch was a waterproof leather bag that never weighed more than twenty pounds. Since every ounce was a drag on the horse, the riders had to weigh under 125 pounds; and they carried only what they needed — horn, pistol, and knife — to defend themselves against attack. Not even a water jug was allowed to add to the load.

It cost five dollars to send a one-half ounce letter by the pony line. That was a lot of money in those days; but despite some complaints, the need was so great that the service had to be doubled from once a week to twice a week. Most writers used thin writing paper and wrote as few words as possible.

7

The riders — all teenagers — faced many dangers as they raced across the western lands. The course was not clearly marked. There was always the danger of enemy attack over the lonely stretches of land. In winter, hungry wolf packs ran across the route, and in the high country there were mountain lions. But records show that in 650,000 miles covered, only one mailbag was ever lost.

The pony riders earned from $100 to $150 a month — very good wages for that time. Their uniform of buckskin jacket, red shirt, bright blue jeans, and black boots made them colorful figures of the time. While the average rider's age was eighteen, some were hired as young as fifteen. They rode as much as eighteen hours a day, riding in rain, snow, or burning desert sun, catching a short nap, then riding on again. The ponies they rode were chosen for speed, courage, and endurance, and were considered to be the finest in the West.

As the danger of the Civil War was foreseen, telegraph lines were pushed rapidly across the country. The wire service began in 1861. It spelled the decline and eventual end of the pony express. The telegraph handled messages more quickly and cheaply. The pony express came to an end eighteen months after it had begun.

8

9. Before the pony express, mail was delivered by _____ .
   A boat
   B railroad
   ● stagecoach
   D telegraph lines

10. Young men probably most wanted to serve as pony express riders because the _____ .
    A job was safe
    ● pay was good
    C hours were short
    D horses were gentle

11. One requirement for being a pony express rider involved _____ .
    ● weight
    B height
    C education
    D experience

12. Pony express riders could best be described as _____ .
    A curious
    B lucky
    ● brave
    D smart

13. The pony express service ended because _____ .
    A there were not enough riders
    ● telegraph service began
    C people could not afford the service
    D there was no need for mail during the Civil War

9

14. Which sentence shows best that the pony express delivery record was good?

● Only one mailbag was ever lost.
B They made it in ten and one-half days.
C They only needed eighty riders.
D It cost five dollars to send a one-half ounce letter.

15. There is enough information in the passage to believe that the pony express was _____.

A ineffective because of the high cost
B unnecessary, but a colorful part of the Old West
C better than the telegraph service that took its place
● fast, efficient, and served the needs of the time

16. Which sentence best sums up the ideas in the passage?

A The pony express failed to meet the needs of the public and was disbanded six months after it began.
● The pony express was started to speed up mail delivery to the Far West, and it ended when telegraph service went into effect.
C The pony express was a cheap and efficient method of delivering mail to the Far West.
D The pony express was an efficient method of mail delivery that took the place of telegraph service in the West.

Name _____

Write a paragraph describing the ideal pony express rider.

_____
_____
_____
_____
_____
_____
_____
_____
_____
_____
_____
_____
_____
_____
_____
_____
_____
_____
_____
_____
_____
_____

10

11

Name _____

Think about the selections you read in "Other Places." Then complete this page. Underline the word or words in the first two items.

1. As you read the selections in this unit, did you picture events and characters in your mind?
   Yes   Sometimes   No

2. How easy or hard were the selections in this unit to read?
   Most were easy.   Most were hard.   All were hard.

3. Write about one or two things that made the selections in this unit easy or hard to enjoy and explain why.
   _____
   _____
   _____

4. List some ways in which you have become a more successful reader this year.
   _____
   _____
   _____

5. Are the selections in this unit the kind that you most like to read? Write a brief explanation telling why or why not.
   _____
   _____
   _____

6. Write about the most interesting thing that you learned in this unit.
   _____
   _____
   _____

13

Harcourt Brace School Publishers • Unit Holistic Reading Assessment

SHADES OF GOLD

Think of another word that is used differently today from the way it was used in the past (for example, "cool," "neat," or "bad"). Explain how the word's meaning has changed.

| UNIT 1 | SCORE: 3 |

In today's society, word meanings have greatly changed. For example, the word "bad" at first only meant something terrible or negative. Now, the same word means that a person, place, object, or event is attractive or fascinating. If I were to use today's meaning of "bad" in a sentence it would go something like this: " That's a 'bad' car!" This is a compliment. It means that I like it. From this, it is abundantly clear to see, "We've come a long way, baby!"

There are more words that are used differently than the ones in the passage. For example the word bad. A long time ago it meant someone who is evil or dishonest. Now it can mean neat or interesting things.

Cool long ago probably meant that it was kind of cold. neat probably ment tidy. Bad probobly meant not good.

Harcourt Brace School Publishers ● Unit Holistic Reading Assessment

Explain why *Bulletin Board* is a good name for the computer program described in this passage.

UNIT 1   SCORE: 3

"Bulletin Board" is a good name for the program because a real bulletin board is for putting messages on it for other people, and that is exactly what this program does.

UNIT 1   SCORE: 2

Because each member leaves measeges.

UNIT 1   SCORE: 1

I think that it is good to have that so they can solve mistories

Explain why the trophy was important to Uncle Hector.

UNIT 2   SCORE: 3

The trophy was important to him because he might have felt he was being forgotten with all the new track champions. Hector also may have wanted his nephews to see it so they would have a goal to spur them on when they tried out for the track team.

UNIT 2   SCORE: 2

I Think That the Trophy was important to uncle Hector. Because he send it in the high pump at his high school.

UNIT 2   SCORE: 1

The trophy was important to uncle Hector because he has collectis trophy's and I he new that he had all of them and he would be a witness.

Harcourt Brace School Publishers • Unit Holistic Reading Assessment

Suppose you didn't have a plastic trash bag to use in making your kite. What could you use in place of a plastic trash bag? Explain why you think so.

UNIT 2   SCORE: 3

If I didn't have a trash bag to make my kite I would use the plastic bags you put your sandwiches + stuff with because then you could feel it up with air attach a string to it and it'll follow along with the wind.

UNIT 2   SCORE: 2

I would use some cloth for clothes + useft for the kite jinsteado fplastic bag.

UNIT 2   SCORE: 1

I would put more sticks so it could fly better.

SHADES OF GOLD

Tell what Kendall was probably thinking when he stopped eating.

UNIT 3   SCORE: 3

  I want to be free. I nkow it is nice here and they really like me, but I want to be free. I must admit theise a lot of things the have to offer here; But they dont have cool, moist, wet, and muddy streams full of larva and rocks or I cant lie down on a wet cool rock on a summers day with the the guys. Then agian I cant eat Hot dogs or turkey slices. And I cant have a cotiowned shoe box bad. Or swing with alison all day on the swing. Or watch tv. I want to be free. I want to be free. I want t be free.

Harcourt Brace School Publishers • Unit Holistic Reading Assessment

UNIT 3 SCORE: 2

He probably was thinking that if
he stoped eating he coutd go free
agin and he coold go live with
oother turtles.

UNIT 3 SCORE: 1

She was probabbly thinking
Kendall was getting sick of meat,
that he wanted something dilfferent
Not hat dogs or turkey.

Use information from the passage to explain how the author feels about war.

UNIT 3 | SCORE: 3

I think that the author doesn't like war, because it said they were assigned to a small tent, it had no flooring, they had food which tasted like dog food.
I think he didn't like war because of the living.

UNIT 3 | SCORE: 2

The author doesn't really like going to war because of the conditions.

UNIT 3 | SCORE: 1

I think the author seems to like war very much because when he came home and told about his many experiences.

Harcourt Brace School Publishers ● Unit Holistic Reading Assessment

Suppose you had a computer like Roger's. Write a paragraph telling how you would use your computer and what you would make it do.

In the following paragraph I am going to tell you how I would use the computer, and what I would make it do. If I had a computer like Roger's I would use it for good things. First of all I would make it destroy the word "fight". This word causes a lot of problems between people and countries. It causes the death of inocent people. Next, I would type all the offensive word on the computer, so we wouldn't have any fights. After that I would make the computer destroy all the names of people that have caused tragedies and deaths of people. So nobody would have a hard time remembering the hardships they went through because of that people. If I had the computer in my hands that's what I would first do.

If I had a computer I would make it do my home work and many other things like make it take away words like homework, clean, room, learn, and school.

"The End"

Harcourt Brace School Publishers • Unit Holistic Reading Assessment

UNIT 4   SCORE: 1

One day my mom and dad went out and bought me my very own computer. I liked this computer I could make it do what I wanted it to do. I made it where I could play any game I wanted too. When I play it I like to play Well Of Fortrun. I like that game it is a very fun game to play. On my computer all you have to do is turn it off by a little botton it turns the monitor and key board part I like my computer very much.

SHADES OF GOLD

How does Dad feel about Goblin? Explain your reasons.

I think Dad really loves Goblin as if he had been Dad's faithful companion since birth. This is because, for one reason he said he liked doing things for Goblin such as grooming or feeding him. For another thing he did these things for Goblin early in the morning before Julie, who was supposed to do the chores anyway, had gotten up. Dad also cares for and loves Goblin, and was a little upset when Julie said she didn't want him to help with Goblin so much anymore. I really do think Dad loves Goblin. So that, of course, is how I think Dad feels about his temporary golden retriever, Goblin.

Harcourt Brace School Publishers • Unit Holistic Reading Assessment

Harcourt Brace School Publishers ● Unit Holistic Reading Assessment

UNIT 4 **SCORE: 2**

Dad likes Goblin because he never had a
dog when he was young and he's usually feeding
him or grooming him.

UNIT 4 **SCORE: 1**

Dad feels ~~angry~~ about ~~Goblin.~~ He
thinks that if Julie feeds Goblin every
time, the dog is going to ~~love~~ her better
than him.

Explain why the dolphins are so important to the Imragen.

UNIT 5 | **SCORE: 3**

Dolfins are so important to the Imragan tribe because the dolfins are what drive the yellow mulet to the people so they dont steasve. If the dolfins wasnt there than the Imragan people would not have very much food unless they sailed off the shore.

UNIT 5 | **SCORE: 2**

They are important because the help them catch fish.

UNIT 5 | **SCORE: 1**

Because Nedo wanted to be with the fisherman and when he was walking the dophin jumped up and started talking to Nedu.

Harcourt Brace School Publishers • Unit Holistic Reading Assessment

Based on what you read in this passage, explain why most of the earth's water cannot be used for drinking.

Most of the earth's water can not be used for drinking because most of the water is not fresh water, it is salt water. There are more salt water oceans, and seas than there are in fresh water lakes, streams and rivers. The water covers 70 percent of the earth's surface and less than 1 percent is fresh water. More than three quarters of fresh water is frozen in the Antartica ice cap.

UNIT 5   SCORE: 2

Most of earth wate can not Be Drank Becuse it is Salt wate and salt isnot good for you But Still habe of earet is salt and hab is Fresn watee youcanprint Fres water.

UNIT 5   SCORE: 1

The earths water can't be used for drinking water because if all the water was drank there would be no homes for fish and animals like frogs and all of them would die and then there would be no water left on the earth.

Harcourt Brace School Publishers • Unit Holistic Reading Assessment

SHADES OF GOLD

Think about the clues the author provided in the story. Then write some of the clues the author gave to make readers think it really was 1814 in the town of Nowhere.

UNIT 6   SCORE: 3

One of the clues is that a sign said, "Nowhere - Population 112." Another clue is that the stores don't take money. The third clue is that the jam, and calendars say 1814. The fourth clue is that they didn't have any cars. The last clue is that they were in costumes about 150 years old.

UNIT 6   SCORE: 2

The calendars
The jar
The clothing
The buildings
No cars,

UNIT 6   SCORE: 1

The jar had a date. Strange clothes.

Write a paragraph describing the ideal pony express rider.

UNIT 6 | **SCORE: 3**

I would describe an ideal pony express rider as one who is brave, and knows how to handle a horse. Someone who is in their teens and weighs under 125 pounds. Someone who knows the route. And someone who knows how to follow directions. And someone who can go without water for a while.

UNIT 6 | **SCORE: 2**

The ideal pony express rider is a strong man that has speed, and is good with horses.

UNIT 6 | **SCORE: 1**

It was good use for when people needed something to be somewhere at a certain date. they will do it for you and it will only cause $6.00

Harcourt Brace School Publishers • Unit Holistic Reading Assessment

Field Test Data

The *Unit Holistic Reading Assessments* were written by professional test-development personnel using specifications based on *Treasury of Literature.* During the fall of 1990, the spring of 1991, and the fall of 1991, test passages and items were field tested. A listing of school test sites that participated in the field tests follows.

Field Test Design

A variety of types of school districts participated in the field tests. They represented different geographic regions of the country, different socioeconomic groups, and different sizes. A few nonpublic schools also participated. Participating students represented a broad range of ability levels.

All tests were administered by regular classroom teachers and returned to the publisher for scoring. Standardized directions were provided for each teacher. Suggested test sittings and approximate testing times were provided; however, teachers were encouraged to allow sufficient time for almost all students to complete the tests.

Although each reading passage and set of comprehension questions was targeted for a particular grade level, the passages and items were tried out at more than one grade level during the field tests to gain a better estimate of item difficulty for students at various grade levels.

Test booklets were returned for scoring and analysis. The item analysis data included the number and percent of students choosing each response option or omitting the item. Point-biserial item discrimination indices were also calculated for each item by grade level. These item-level statistics formed the primary sets of data used to select the final passages and items and to make appropriate item revisions.

Each participating teacher also completed a questionnaire indicating the appropriateness of the passages and items, the interest level of the materials, and the clarity of the directions.

Based on the field test data, the final *Unit Holistic Reading Assessments* were built by the publisher.

Aberdeen, SD	Land O'Lakes, FL
Bossier City, LA	Lockhart, TX
Brooklyn, NY	Mahomet, IL
Cabot, AR	McAllen, TX
Chaparral, NM	Moreno Valley, CA
Conway, AR	Nashville, TN
Corsicana, TX	New Carlisle, OH
Donnellson, IA	North Bergen, NJ
Dry Fork, VA	North Huntingdon, PA
Everett, WA	Phoenix, AZ
Fairless Hills, PA	Portland, OR
Grand Prairie, TX	San Antonio, TX
Greer, SC	University Heights, OH
Houston, TX	Vancouver, WA
Kansas City, KS	Vinemont, AL
Katy, TX	

Answer Keys for the Multiple-choice Items

UNIT					
1	**2**	**3**	**4**	**5**	**6**
1. A	1. B	1. B	1. B	1. B	1. B
2. B	2. A	2. A	2. C	2. D	2. D
3. C	3. C	3. C	3. B	3. A	3. A
4. A	4. A	4. B	4. A	4. C	4. C
5. B	5. D	5. D	5. D	5. B	5. B
6. A	6. C	6. C	6. A	6. C	6. A
7. C	7. A	7. A	7. C	7. D	7. C
8. B	8. C	8. B	8. B	8. A	8. A
9. B	9. C	9. C	9. C	9. C	9. C
10. C	10. A	10. B	10. B	10. B	10. B
11. A	11. B	11. D	11. B	11. A	11. A
12. B	12. A	12. B	12. C	12. D	12. C
13. C	13. B	13. C	13. A	13. A	13. B
14. D	14. C	14. A	14. C	14. C	14. A
15. A	15. D	15. B	15. B	15. B	15. D
16. D	16. A	16. A	16. A	16. A	16. B

Harcourt Brace School Publishers • Unit Holistic Reading Assessment

Treasury of Literature
Unit Holistic Reading Assessment
Class Record Form

Teacher _____

School _____

Student Name	UNIT 1		UNIT 2		UNIT 3	
	Multiple-choice / Writing	Date _____ Comments	Multiple-choice / Writing	Date _____ Comments	Multiple-choice / Writing	Date _____ Comments

Treasury of Literature
Unit Holistic Reading Assessment
Class Record Form

Teacher _____

School _____

Student Name	UNIT 4 Multiple-choice / Writing	Date _____ Comments	UNIT 5 Multiple-choice / Writing	Date _____ Comments	UNIT 6 Multiple-choice / Writing	Date _____ Comments

Harcourt Brace School Publishers • Unit Holistic Reading Assessment

Unit Holistic Reading Assessment
UNIT ONE

SHADES OF GOLD

SUMMARY OF PERFORMANCE

NAME _____ DATE _____

MULTIPLE-CHOICE ITEMS

VERY GOOD READER	AVERAGE READER	FAIR READER	POOR READER	PUPIL SCORE	COMMENTS
15-16	13-14	11-12	10 OR LESS	____	_____

OPEN-ENDED ITEMS

EXCELLENT	ADEQUATE	UNSATISFACTORY	NONSCORABLE
3	2	1	NS

QUESTION 1   ____ _____

QUESTION 2   ____ _____

SELF-ASSESSMENT

COMMENTS _____

_____

Printed in the United States of America

Illustrations: Polly Lewis/Philip M. Veloric—Artist's Representative, p. 2; Len Ebert/Philip M. Veloric—Artist's Representative, p. 7.

ISBN 0-15-305454-9

1 2 3 4 5 6 7 8 9 10   073   97   96   95   94

On Being Silly

Directions: *Read each story and the questions that follow. Fill in the answer circle in front of the correct answer for each question.*

How have the meanings of words changed?

How would you feel if someone called you "silly"? Would you think that person was paying you a compliment or insulting you? If you are like most people, you would take the remark as an insult. It might hurt your feelings or make you angry. However, long ago the same comment would have probably meant something very different to people. At one time rich people were called "silly" because they didn't have to work if they did not want to. The word "silly" was understood to mean "lucky" or "blessed." Later on people came to think that it was a good thing to work, and the word "silly" came to mean "does nothing." A "silly" person was considered lazy, helpless, weak, or useless. Today, when we call a person or an idea "silly," we put down that person or idea.

In a similar way, the word "amusing" was once used very differently from the way it is used today. If we say that a book or movie is "amusing," we probably mean that it is funny or entertaining. The word sounds like a compliment. Yet there was a time when "amusing" people more commonly meant distracting their attention so that they could be deceived or tricked. A pickpocket, for example, might "amuse" a person while his partner stole the victim's wallet.

Another word that has changed considerably is "awesome." Many people use it today to describe something that is so great that it overwhelms us. We admire things that are awesome today,

Harcourt Brace School Publishers • Unit Holistic Reading Assessment

  1

although our admiration may also contain a little bit of wonder and even disbelief or fear. This last sense was once the main meaning of the word. People called something "awesome" if it filled them with fear and terror. An erupting volcano, for example, was considered "awesome" back then. But a day off from school was not considered "awesome"!

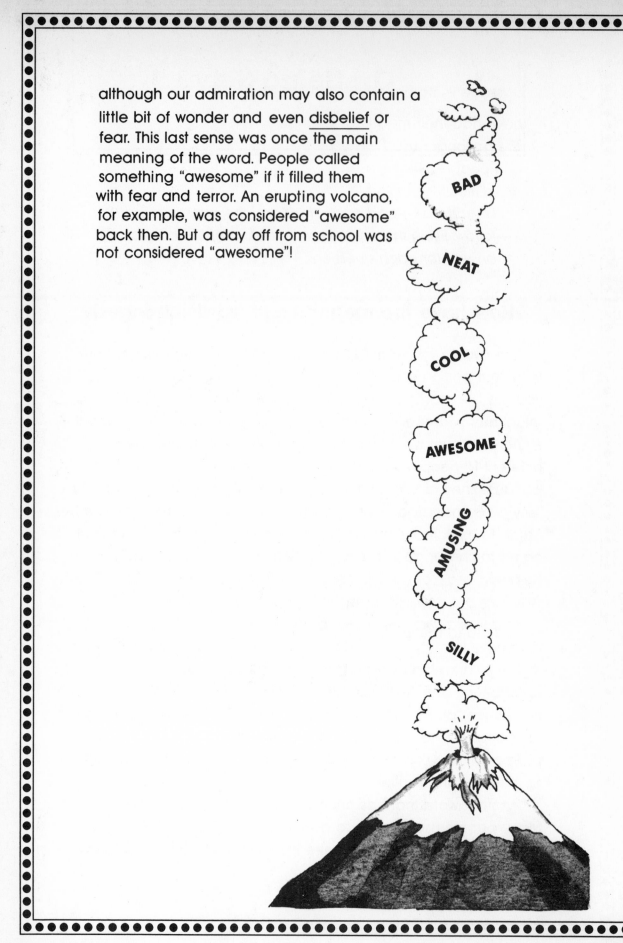

BAD

NEAT

COOL

AWESOME

AMUSING

SILLY

Harcourt Brace School Publishers • Unit Holistic Reading Assessment

Go on

1. This passage is mainly about words that _____ .

    (A) have had their meanings changed

    (B) are no longer used

    (C) hurt people's feelings

    (D) are difficult to explain

2. This passage was written mainly to _____ .

    (A) praise

    (B) inform

    (C) warn

    (D) persuade

3. A person who was called "silly" long ago probably had a lot of _____ .

    (A) jobs

    (B) courage

    (C) money

    (D) friends

4. Long ago, the words "silly" and "amusing" both _____ .

    (A) had meanings different from their meanings today

    (B) meant almost exactly the same thing

    (C) described the work a person did

    (D) were taken as insults

Harcourt Brace School Publishers • Unit Holistic Reading Assessment

5. The word <u>disbelief</u> in the passage means _____ .

    (A) a strong opinion about something

    (B) a feeling that something is not true

    (C) an idea that something is sure to happen

    (D) an idea accepted as truth

6. Which of these would have been called "amusing" long ago?

    (A) a dishonest storekeeper

    (B) a funny story

    (C) a powerful volcano

    (D) a rich man

7. The author of this passage probably _____ .

    (A) likes to insult people

    (B) speaks more than one language

    (C) studies words

    (D) lived long ago

8. Many of the words in this article are in quotation marks because _____ .

    (A) they are titles

    (B) they are being explained

    (C) someone is saying them

    (D) they are difficult to understand

Harcourt Brace School Publishers • Unit Holistic Reading Assessment

Stop

Name _____

Think of another word that is used differently today from the way it was used in the past (for example, "cool," "neat," or "bad"). Explain how the word's meaning has changed.

_____

_____

_____

_____

_____

_____

_____

_____

_____

_____

_____

_____

_____

_____

_____

_____

Harcourt Brace School Publishers • Unit Holistic Reading Assessment

Getting the Message

How does *Bulletin Board* work?

Carrie went to the school's computer room to use the new *Bulletin Board* program, which allows students from several schools to communicate by computer. At first the screen on her computer displayed a menu, a list of the different programs she could choose from. To select the *Bulletin Board* program, Carrie moved the blinking square, called the *cursor*, to the words *Bulletin Board*. Then she pressed the key that said "Enter." In a matter of seconds, the menu disappeared, and the screen said:

> Welcome to *Bulletin Board*.
>
> What is your name? >

Carrie typed in her name and pressed the "Enter" key again. The screen said:

> Welcome to *Bulletin Board*.
>
> What is your name? >Carrie Jefferson
> What is the name of your school? >

Carrie typed in the name of her school, then pressed "Enter" again, and the screen said:

Harcourt Brace School Publishers • Unit Holistic Reading Assessment

> Welcome to *Bulletin Board.*
>
> What is your name? >Carrie Jefferson
> What is the name of your school? >Westerville
> What is your password? >

Carrie typed "Friday" and then pressed the "Enter" key, but the word "Friday" did not appear on the screen, where other people could see it. Only Carrie and the computer knew the password she had chosen the day she joined the *Bulletin Board* group. Each student's password was kept secret. A student who did not have a password the computer would recognize could not get into the *Bulletin Board* program.

Now the screen showed a menu that said:

> What would you like to do, Carrie Jefferson?
> S = Send a message
> Rn = Read new messages
> Ra = Read all messages
> E = Exit from *Bulletin Board*

Carrie typed "Rn" and then pressed "Enter." In a moment the screen said:

> To: Everyone
> I had a great vacation. How about the rest of you Bozos?
>
> Red
>
> To: Red
> Who are you calling Bozo, you Bozo? I'm no clown! I'm taking eighth-grade math even though I'm only in sixth grade. By the way, has anyone in Mr. Wallace's class at Southside Middle School finished problem number four on tonight's homework? What answer did you get?
>
> Joe Einstein

To: Joe Einstein

You *are* a Bozo! Who cares if you skipped a grade
in math? Math isn't everything. Why don't you get
a life! And if you're so smart, do problem number
four yourself.

                                        Chrissy

To: Everyone

There will be a city wide clothing drive next Saturday.
Students from Westerville, Southside, and Central are
all asked to help out. Meet in the school cafeteria
at 9:00 a.m. Bring clothing that you no longer need.
Be sure it is clean and in good repair.
                    LAST NEW MESSAGE
            TO EXIT, TYPE "M" FOR MENU

Carrie typed "M" and pressed "Enter." Then she typed "S."
A moment later the screen said:

            Whom do you want to address? >
            What is your message? >

Carrie typed "Everyone," and her message and then pressed
"Enter." The screen said:

To: Everyone

Please use the *Bulletin Board* properly, or the
teachers may take it off the system. My class was
warned about calling each other names and
sharing answers to homework problems. I'm sure the
rest of you have heard the rules, too. Also, who left
the message about the clothing drive? You forgot to
say *which* school cafeteria to meet in.

                            Carrie of Westerville

Harcourt Brace School Publishers • Unit Holistic Reading Assessment

9. This passage is mainly about _____ .

(A) Carrie's day at school

(B) a computerized message system

(C) how to use a computer

(D) an argument among some computer users

10. The <u>password</u> each student has is a kind of a _____ .

(A) message from a teacher

(B) signature to put at the end of a message

(C) secret code to enter the program

(D) special word that tells about that person

11. What should Carrie type if she wants to read all of the messages students have left?

(A) Ra

(B) Rn

(C) S

(D) E

12. Which term best describes Joe Einstein?

(A) polite

(B) show-off

(C) brilliant

(D) hardworking

Go on

13. The tone of the message Red left is _____ .

  (A) mysterious
  (B) scary
  (C) rude
  (D) serious

14. Chrissy appears to dislike _____ .

  (A) Red
  (B) Carrie
  (C) Mr. Wallace
  (D) Joe Einstein

15. The message that Carrie leaves is a kind of _____ .

  (A) scolding
  (B) story
  (C) joke
  (D) puzzle

16. Which of the following is a **fact** from the passage?

  (A) You *are* a Bozo!
  (B) I had a great vacation.
  (C) Math isn't everything.
  (D) Each student's password was kept secret.

Name _____

Explain why *Bulletin Board* is a good name for the computer program described in this passage.

_____

_____

_____

_____

_____

_____

_____

_____

_____

_____

_____

_____

_____

_____

_____

_____

_____

_____

Harcourt Brace School Publishers • Unit Holistic Reading Assessment

Name _____

Think about the selections you read in "Surprises." Then complete this page. Underline the word or words in the first two items.

1. Did you enjoy reading about the things that happened in the selections in this unit?

   Yes   Sometimes   No

2. Were you able to understand all the words used in these selections?

   Yes   Most of the time   No

3. Write briefly about one thing that made reading these selections hard or one thing that made reading them easy.

   _____

   _____

   _____

4. Which selection had the most new information? Write and explain why.

   _____

   _____

   _____

5. If you could read more selections like one in this unit, which one would you choose? Write and tell why.

   _____

   _____

6. Which of the selections in this unit do you think you will remember? Explain why.

   _____

   _____

   _____

TREASURY OF LITERATURE
SHADES OF GOLD
Unit Holistic Reading Assessment
Unit One

HARCOURT
BRACE

Orlando   Atlanta   Austin   Boston   San Francisco   Chicago   Dallas   New York
Toronto   London

PART NO. 9997-09833-1

ISBN 0-15-305454-9 (12 OF EACH UNIT TEST)

6

SHADES OF GOLD

TREASURY OF LITERATURE

SUMMARY OF PERFORMANCE

NAME_____ DATE_____

MULTIPLE-CHOICE ITEMS

VERY GOOD READER	AVERAGE READER	FAIR READER	POOR READER	PUPIL SCORE	COMMENTS
15-16	13-14	11-12	10 OR LESS	____	_____

OPEN-ENDED ITEMS

EXCELLENT	ADEQUATE	UNSATISFACTORY	NONSCORABLE
3	2	1	NS

QUESTION 1   ____   _____

QUESTION 2   ____   _____

SELF-ASSESSMENT

COMMENTS   _____

                _____

Illustrations: Dee de Rosa/Carol Bancroft & Friends—Artist's Representative, p. 2; Don Dyen/Philip M. Veloric—
Artist's Representative, p. 6–8.

Printed in the United States of America

ISBN 0-15-305454-9

1 2 3 4 5 6 7 8 9 10   073   97   96   95   94

Trophy "Case"

Directions: Read each story and the questions that follow. Fill in the answer circle in front of the correct answer for each question.

Is Uncle Hector telling the truth?

Uncle Hector was really proud that he had been a tri-state champion in the high jump when he was a seventh grader. When his nephews, Lucas and Juan, went out for track, Uncle Hector insisted they tell their coach that their uncle was <u>formerly</u> a champion. "Show him my team's 1972 trophy in the case," he said.

It seemed really important to Hector that he be remembered. So Juan went by the trophy case in the main hall at Adams Middle School to check on Uncle Hector's team trophy. He looked and looked, trying to read the engraved names and dates on the track trophies.

Juan couldn't find any trophies for any sport for the year 1971 or 1972. The dates on the trophy <u>collection</u> jumped from 1970 to 1973. "Uncle Hector

must be mistaken," he told Lucas. "It doesn't look like the school had any good athletes at all those two years."

"He's probably living in a fantasy world," Lucas said.

The boys decided to have Uncle Hector prove his great abilities in high-jumping — not by actually jumping, of course, since he was now an old man in his thirties. Instead, they asked him to go home and get the individual trophy he claimed to have won. "Can't," Uncle Hector said glumly. "It got tossed out somehow while I was away in the Marines." The boys let that go without a comment, afraid that he might start telling his Marine stories again.

At Uncle Hector's insistence, Lucas asked his principal, Mr. Taggers, about the trophies. Mr. Taggers pointed out that before

1973, there was no Adams Middle School — that Uncle Hector had attended Harrison Junior High. "The Harrison trophy case was moved to the high-school building after 1970 while this building was being remodeled. Any trophies won during that time should be over there," he said.

Solving the mystery of Uncle Hector's missing trophy became a genuine challenge for Lucas and Juan. They found no Harrison trophies at the high school, either. The high-school track coach said he thought the junior-high trophies for 1971 and 1972 had been given to the Harrison County Historical Society Museum in 1973. "The remodeling at the other building was finished," he said, "and the junior-high kids were moved back there to start the newly renamed Adams Middle School."

At the museum, the boys were directed to an old glass storage case in the basement. It was so dusty they could hardly see into it, but there sat the Harrison Junior High trophies for 1971 and 1972. Yet there was no tri-state championship trophy for track in 1972! "Gosh!" Juan said. "Uncle Hector will be so disappointed."

"I think he knows what to expect!" Lucas grumbled.

"Did you find what you were looking for?" the white-haired museum director asked.

"No," Juan said sadly.

"Funny," the man said. "No one's asked about those trophies in all the years we've had them. Now yours was the second request to see them today. The other fellow asked to borrow one, and I let him take it."

"Was his name Hector Cruz?" Juan asked hopefully.

"Well," the man said, searching in the pocket of his sweater for a piece of paper, "seems to me that it was."

Go on

1. This story is mostly about two boys who _____ .

   (A) win a track trophy and donate it to a historical museum
   (B) search for a missing trophy because their uncle claims he won it
   (C) search for a trophy so that their school collection will be complete
   (D) go out for track and brag to their coach about their uncle's trophy

2. In this story the word collection means _____ .

   (A) an accumulation of similar things
   (B) the act of picking something up
   (C) a set of items for sale in a specific season
   (D) things that have been donated

3. The word formerly in the story means _____ .

   (A) well shaped
   (B) lacking structure
   (C) at an earlier time
   (D) in an orderly fashion

4. Why does Juan try so hard to locate the trophy?

   (A) The trophy means a lot to Uncle Hector.
   (B) He wants to keep the trophy.
   (C) He wants to show the trophy to his classmates.
   (D) He thinks the search is a lot of fun.

Harcourt Brace School Publishers • Unit Holistic Reading Assessment

5. When they found no trophy at Adams Middle School, Lucas and Juan probably felt _____ .

(A) frightened

(B) relieved

(C) lucky

(D) disappointed

6. The boys were having trouble finding the trophy because it _____ .

(A) had been thrown away

(B) was completely covered with dust

(C) had been moved so many times

(D) never really existed

7. Which of these is a **fact** from the story?

(A) They found no Harrison trophies at the high school.

(B) He's probably living in a fantasy world.

(C) It seemed really important to Hector that he be remembered.

(D) Uncle Hector will be so disappointed.

8. This story is most like a _____ .

(A) news story

(B) history

(C) mystery

(D) comedy

Stop

Name _____

Explain why the trophy was important to Uncle Hector.

_____

_____

_____

_____

_____

_____

_____

_____

_____

_____

_____

_____

_____

_____

_____

_____

_____

_____

_____

_____

Stop

Go Fly a Kite!

What do you need to make a kite?

When windy weather arrives, everyone feels inclined to accept the suggestion to "go fly a kite!" If you don't happen to have a kite, it's possible to make one from materials that are likely to be found in and around your home.

What You Need

Start with a large plastic trash bag. It must be at least 24 inches long and 16 inches wide. You also need two sticks or kite dowels. Each of them should be 24 inches long and 3/16 inch wide. They can have round or square edges. If you want to use kite dowels, you can get them at a kite store, toy store, or hardware store.

You will also need the following:

- paper
- ruler
- pen, marker, or chalk
- scissors
- glue
- tape
- hole puncher
- string

Optional:
- cloth or plastic for a tail

Harcourt Brace School Publishers • Unit Holistic Reading Assessment

Go on

Directions

1. *Make a pattern.*

First, use a large sheet of paper and a ruler to make a pattern like the one shown in Diagram 1. The pattern will be placed on the plastic trash bag, and you will trace around it to cut your kite in the right shape. Lay the trash bag on a flat surface; turn the bag so that a long edge is at the bottom. Finally, place the pattern on the bag and use a pen, marker, or chalk to trace around it on the bag.

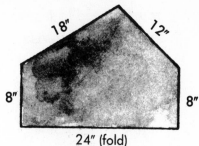

24" (fold)
Diagram 1

2. *Cut out the kite and attach sticks.*

Cut around the pattern shape you traced, making sure to go through both sides of the bag. Do **not** cut along the 24-inch fold. Unfold the trash bag, and you will see that you have a whole kite. Glue the dowels to the kite as shown in Diagram 2. Let the glue dry, and then tape the dowels in place to make sure the sticks won't fall off.

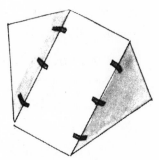

Diagram 2

3. *Make and attach the bridle.*

The long kite-flying string must be attached to a <u>bridle</u>, or rigging. To make the bridle, cut a piece of string 6 feet long. Put tape on the two points of the flaps to <u>reinforce</u> them so they won't tear. Using scissors or a hole puncher, punch a hole through each of the two taped points. Tie one end of the bridle string through one hole, and tie the other end through the other hole. Look at Diagram 3 if you are not sure how to do this.

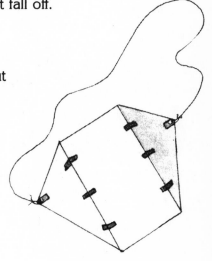

Diagram 3

Harcourt Brace School Publishers • Unit Holistic Reading Assessment

Go on

4. Attach a kite-flying string.

You will need to fasten a kite-flying string to the center of the
bridle; be sure to use a very long string so that your kite can fly
high. To find the center of the bridle,
bring the kite flaps exactly together.
Keeping the flaps together, pull
up the bridle. Use a pen to make
a mark on the string right in the
center. Attach the string to the
center of the bridle as shown in
Diagram 4. Tie it with a very
tight knot.

5. Make a tail.

It's possible to fly your kite without a tail,
but if there is a very strong wind, a tail will
help keep the kite upright and well balanced.
A tail can be made from a thin 4-foot strip cut
from cloth or a plastic trash bag. Use 3-inch lengths of string to
tie knots every 6 inches along the strip; this will give the tail weight
and will help balance the kite. The tail can be attached with safety
pins, tape, or staples or by sewing. It should be centered at the
bottom of the kite.

Diagram 4

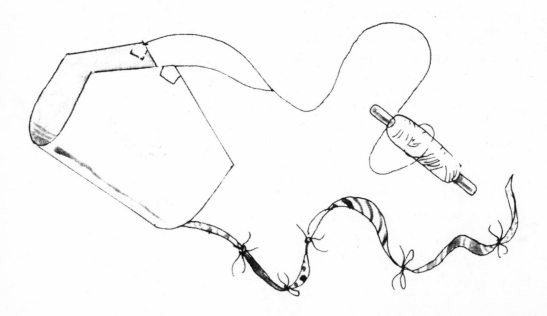

Go on

9. This passage mostly gives information about how to _____ .

(A) decorate a kite

(B) make a kite pattern

(C) make a kite of your own

(D) attach a tail to a kite

10. In the directions a bridle is _____ .

(A) a string connected to two sides of a kite

(B) part of a horse's rein or harness

(C) a wedding bouquet

(D) a cross stick on a kite

11. Kite dowels are _____ .

(A) tails

(B) sticks

(C) strings

(D) bridles

12. The kite-flying string has to be tied to the _____ .

(A) bridle

(B) kite dowels

(C) tail

(D) pattern

13. The word <u>reinforce</u> in the passage means _____ .

  (A) draw attention to
  (B) strengthen
  (C) resist again
  (D) encourage

14. The kite is probably made from a plastic trash bag rather than cardboard because the _____ .

  (A) cardboard is harder to cut
  (B) cardboard won't bend easily
  (C) trash bag weighs less
  (D) trash bag is less likely to tear

15. The information in this passage is mostly presented as a _____ .

  (A) list of reasons
  (B) story
  (C) comparison of ideas
  (D) sequence of steps

16. In which book is this passage most likely to be found?

  (A) *Do-It-Yourself Projects*
  (B) *An Expert's Guide to Aircraft*
  (C) *Poems About Kites, Birds, and Butterflies*
  (D) *The History of Flight*

Harcourt Brace School Publishers • Unit Holistic Reading Assessment

Stop

Name _____

Suppose you didn't have a plastic trash bag to use in making your kite. What could you use in place of a plastic trash bag? Explain why you think so.

_____

_____

_____

_____

_____

_____

_____

_____

_____

_____

_____

_____

_____

_____

_____

_____

_____

_____

Harcourt Brace School Publishers • Unit Holistic Reading Assessment

Name _____

Think about the selections you read in "Heroes." Then complete this page. Underline the word or words in the first two items.

1. As you read these selections, could you see in your mind what was happening?

   Yes   Sometimes   No

2. How well did these selections hold your attention?

   Very well   Fairly well   Not well

3. Write a brief explanation and tell why some selections did or did not hold your attention.

   _____

   _____

   _____

4. List some ways you think you could become a better reader.

   _____

   _____

   _____

5. Which character in a selection in this unit did you particularly like or dislike? Tell why.

   _____

   _____

   _____

6. Which of the selections in this unit do you think would make the best movie? Tell why.

   _____

   _____

   _____

Harcourt Brace School Publishers • Unit Holistic Reading Assessment

TREASURY OF LITERATURE
SHADES OF GOLD
UNIT HOLISTIC READING ASSESSMENT
UNIT TWO

HARCOURT
BRACE

**Orlando Atlanta Austin Boston San Francisco Chicago Dallas New York
Toronto London**

PART NO. 9997-09834-X

ISBN 0-15-305454-9 (12 OF EACH UNIT TEST)

UNIT HOLISTIC
READING ASSESSMENT
UNIT THREE

SHADES OF GOLD

SUMMARY OF PERFORMANCE

NAME_____   DATE_____

MULTIPLE-CHOICE ITEMS

VERY GOOD READER	AVERAGE READER	FAIR READER	POOR READER	PUPIL SCORE	COMMENTS
15-16	13-14	11-12	10 OR LESS	____	_____

OPEN-ENDED ITEMS

EXCELLENT	ADEQUATE	UNSATISFACTORY	NONSCORABLE
3	2	1	NS

QUESTION 1   ____   _____

QUESTION 2   ____   _____

SELF-ASSESSMENT

COMMENTS   _____

_____

Grateful acknowledgment is made to The Herald-Times for permission to reprint "Turtle Teaches Girl Love's Bittersweet Lesson" (Retitled: "Kendall Goes Free") from *The Herald-Times*, October 9, 1990. Text copyright © 1990 by The Herald-Times.

Illustrations: Eldon Doty/HK Portfolio–Artist's Representative, p. 1; Polly Lewis/Philip M. Veloric–Artist's Representative, p. 7.

Printed in the United States of America

ISBN 0-15-305454-9

1 2 3 4 5 6 7 8 9 10   073   97   96   95   94

Kendall Goes Free

by Dann Denny

Directions: *Read each story and the questions that follow. Fill in the answer circle in front of the correct answer for each question.*

How does Alison feel about giving up her pet?

This summer, on her 7th birthday, our first-born daughter received the most thrilling gift of her life — a box turtle.

Alison's face lit up like a sunrise when this sluggish, dome-backed reptile was placed into her hands. She named him Kendall, and talked to him as a mother would a child.

"Oh Kendall," she would say, holding him to her face and pressing her nose against his. "You're such a sweetheart."

Compared to most reptiles, Kendall enjoyed a regal lifestyle. I built for him a lavish villa. It was a 4- by 6-foot wooden box — complete with swimming pool, sandy beach area, and shoebox bed. He dined on hotdogs and sliced turkey.

If Kendall was not <u>luxuriating</u> in his home, he was with Alison. When she lay on the couch and watched TV, she would place Kendall on her chest and gently stroke the back of his neck with her finger. When she swooped back and forth on her tree swing, Kendall would ride in her lap.

Eventually, she coaxed Kendall to snatch pieces of hotdog from her hand. With the meat in his mouth, he often would burrow beneath a blanket or bed pillow, concealing all but his stubby tail.

"Silly Kendall," she would say with a giggle. "You're not very good at playing hide and seek."

But all was not bliss. In the late evening, my wife and I could hear Kendall's claws scratching against the walls of his home. He

Harcourt Brace School Publishers • Unit Holistic Reading Assessment

would pull himself upright, then topple over onto his back with a loud *thud*. Undeterred, he would try — again and again — to scale his way to freedom.

As we listened, we realized Kendall would have to go. The question was when. Fortunately, Kendall gave us the answer. He stopped eating.

"Daddy, you have to call a veterinarian right away," said Alison when she noticed the chunks of uneaten meat in Kendall's home. "He's sick."

"He's not sick," I told her. "Kendall wants to be free. He loves you, but he wants to be free."

The next day, in the early evening, Alison and I went to a small creek that winds its way lazily through some woodlands behind a neighborhood park. The air was heavy, and the first shadows of dusk were beginning to slant across the water.

Cradling Kendall in her hands, Alison tiptoed through some inch-deep water onto an island of smooth rocks. She lifted him to her face and kissed him on the nose.

"Goodbye, sweetheart. I love you."

Forcing a tight-lipped smile, she gently laid him in the shallow stream. As her fingers pulled away, Kendall lay motionless in the water, his legs dangling limply by his sides as the current carried him slowly downstream.

Suddenly, his neck shot up like a periscope. As his eyes scanned his boundless surroundings and his pinhead-sized nostrils smelled the rich aroma of freedom, Kendall's webbed feet began to paddle.

Alison's face grew taut as she watched him churn toward the opposite side of the stream.

"Goodbye, Kendall. I love you," she called out. "I'll never forget you. Never ever."

Kendall climbed out of the water, clambered up a muddy bank and disappeared into a patch of tall grass.

I glanced at Alison's face. She was staring vacantly at the bank, her eyes locked on the grassy area where Kendall had vanished from sight.

"Are you sure he'll be all right, Daddy?" she asked.

"Yes, he'll be fine."

"And happy?"

"Very."

She shrugged her shoulders and heaved a big sigh. Then, after several moments of silence, her face brightened.

"Hey, I've got a great idea," she said, a trace of excitement returning to her voice. "Let's collect some of these shiny rocks."

1. The person who is telling this story is _____ .

   (A) Alison
   (B) Alison's father
   (C) Alison's mother
   (D) a reporter

2. In this story the word scale means _____ .

   (A) climb
   (B) clean
   (C) a turtle's skin
   (D) machine used to weigh something

3. The word luxuriating in this story means _____ .

   (A) spending a lot of money
   (B) growing bigger and bigger
   (C) enjoying a good life
   (D) staying very healthy

4. What caused Alison to think that Kendall was sick?

   (A) He lay motionless in the water.
   (B) He stopped eating.
   (C) He hid under a blanket.
   (D) He ate from her hand.

Harcourt Brace School Publishers • Unit Holistic Reading Assessment

Go on

5. Alison and her father put Kendall into the stream because they _____ .

   (A) no longer wanted to take care of him
   (B) wanted to see if he could swim
   (C) wanted him to clean himself
   (D) thought that was best for him

6. What finally became of Kendall?

   (A) He returned to Alison's yard.
   (B) He drowned in the stream.
   (C) He became a free turtle.
   (D) He got lost in the tall grass.

7. At the end of the story, Alison seems to believe that _____ .

   (A) a free life will be best for Kendall
   (B) her father made the wrong decision about Kendall
   (C) Kendall needs some real rocks in his box at home
   (D) she can come and see Kendall when she wants

8. What lesson does the author of this story probably want to teach us?

   (A) Hotdogs aren't good for turtles to eat.
   (B) Wild animals should not be kept as pets.
   (C) Children should obey their parents.
   (D) Children should be taught how to name their pets.

Name _____

Tell what Kendall was probably thinking when he stopped eating.

_____

_____

_____

_____

_____

_____

_____

_____

_____

_____

_____

_____

_____

_____

_____

_____

_____

_____

Harcourt Brace School Publishers • Unit Holistic Reading Assessment

Stop

The Hump

What was life like for these pilots?

During the war between the United States and Japan, pilots in the U.S. Army Air Corps flew supplies from India into China using C-47s and C-46s, two-engine transport planes. The Himalayas, parallel chains of mountains between India and China, include some of the tallest peaks in the world and were known to these men as "The Hump."

Years after the war was over, the Air Force mailed the diary of one of these pilots to his family. From it they learned more about the mission, the camp where the men lived, and one way that the men passed their free time.

OCT. 24, 1943

The Hump is wild, beautiful, and majestic. It is certainly the most difficult territory in the world. Many of the peaks we fly over reach up to 17,000 and 18,000 feet above sea level. At night, we take a direct route into China, right over two Japanese airfields. We are unarmed and unescorted by our fighter planes, and we carry gasoline as cargo. Too frequently, our planes, especially C-46s, are shot down or crash into the mountains.

This is tropical country, and our runways are set right in a jungle of brush. The airfield is in a valley between two of the mountain ranges. Anti-aircraft guns poke their mean-looking snouts up from various posts.

War is a serious business here; this field has suffered bomb raids. Japanese outposts and fields are only fifty miles away. Deep slit-trenches are provided for us to dive into during air raids. We wear our army automatic pistols and keep our gas masks and helmets close by at all times.

During a recent bombing alert, I stayed in the mess tent long enough to eat several desserts left behind by my buddies who quickly took cover. Enlisted men eat their meals outdoors out of mess kits. We officers eat inside on plates. The food is not so hot. Tonight "C rations" were served. I think they must taste like dog food.

We are assigned to a small tent with no flooring, and we sleep on army canvas cots — no sheets and no pillows or mattresses; just two blankets. By morning, I nearly freeze. The other day, I cut down some bamboo and made a clothes-rail, and a rack for our baggage. We have an outside latrine, located by a big banana tree.

Oct. 25, 1943

We have a regular menagerie here. Immediately back of our tents are two monkeys. About fifty yards down the way, one of the boys has a tame leopard. He raised it from a cub. I was playing with it today, but it plays too rough.

We visited a private about a mile from here whose hobby is catching and raising snakes found in this region. He has several pythons, one of them eleven feet in length. Running around loose on the floor were two lizards some eighteen inches long.

When we entered, the private was busily engaged in trying to induce one of some ten-odd snakes in one cage to eat a white mouse. The mouse either had a charmed life, or the reptiles weren't hungry. Several snakes got into a fight, and the private had to open their mouths and pry them loose. One snake in this cage was a tree snake, whose chief claim to fame is his ability to flatten his body and glide through the air from one tree to another.

In another cage were four or five species of deadly poisonous vipers. In still another, there were six cobras. Reaching into this cage, the private pulled out a large snake and pried its mouth open. Pushing gently on one of its extended fangs, he caused several drops of deadly venom to ooze out onto his fingernail. Assuring me that the snake rarely struck and that he had been bitten only twenty-one times since he started collecting snakes, he placed the snake in my hands. I was a bit <u>skeptical</u>, especially so when it spread its hood and, with forked tongue darting energetically in and out, began weaving its head about six inches in front of my face.

The private explained how he gets most of the venom out of his body when he is bitten. He handles all of his snakes freely and without fear, claiming that any snake could become accustomed to handling in several hours. Maybe so.

Harcourt Brace School Publishers • Unit Holistic Reading Assessment

9. The October 24 and 25 entries in this diary are mostly about a transport pilot's _____ .

(A) description of flying battles he experienced during a war
(B) account of Japanese air strength at the beginning of a war
(C) mission and camp life during a war
(D) memories of his buddies after a war

10. The introduction to the passage tells us all of the following information **except** _____ .

(A) where the pilot flew
(B) the name of the pilot
(C) the pilots' nickname for the mountains
(D) the type of plane the pilot flew

11. The word <u>unarmed</u> in this passage means _____ .

(A) ready for battle
(B) not threatened
(C) missing some limbs
(D) without weapons

12. The diary suggests that the Himalayas are _____ .

(A) ugly and frightening
(B) wild but beautiful
(C) tame and boring
(D) low but dangerous

13. As it is described here, life in the tents seems _____ .

(A) relaxing

(B) luxurious

(C) uncomfortable

(D) unexciting

14. Which sentence best summarizes how the pilot probably felt about life in the camp?

(A) He did not enjoy it but tried to make the best of it.

(B) He thought of it as a really worthwhile experience.

(C) He disliked it, so he gave up trying.

(D) He was lonely and wanted to go home.

15. The word skeptical in this passage means _____ .

(A) angry

(B) doubting

(C) amused

(D) trusting

16. If you were to fly over the Himalayas today, you would be most certain to see _____ .

(A) high mountains

(B) tame leopards

(C) vipers in cages

(D) transport airplanes

Harcourt Brace School Publishers • Unit Holistic Reading Assessment

Stop

Name _____

Use information from the passage to explain how the author feels about war.

_____

_____

_____

_____

_____

_____

_____

_____

_____

_____

_____

_____

_____

_____

_____

_____

_____

_____

Harcourt Brace School Publishers • Unit Holistic Reading Assessment

Name _____

Think about the selections you read in "A World Away." Then complete this page. Underline the word or words in the first two items.

1. Would you look for selections like these to read on your own?
   Yes   Maybe   No

2. Were you able to understand the vocabulary in these selections?
   Yes   Most of the time   No

3. Write about the most interesting thing you learned in this unit.

   _____

   _____

   _____

4. Do you read more or less now than you have in the past? Write and tell what would make you read more.

   _____

   _____

   _____

5. Choose the selection you liked most or least in this unit. Write your feelings about it.

   _____

   _____

   _____

6. In which of the places described in the unit's selections would you choose to live? Explain your choices.

   _____

   _____

   _____

Harcourt Brace School Publishers • Unit Holistic Reading Assessment

TREASURY OF LITERATURE
SHADES OF GOLD
Unit Holistic Reading Assessment
Unit Three

HARCOURT
BRACE

**Orlando Atlanta Austin Boston San Francisco Chicago Dallas New York
Toronto London**

PART NO. 9997-09835-8

ISBN 0-15-305454-9 (12 OF EACH UNIT TEST)

UNIT HOLISTIC
READING ASSESSMENT
UNIT FOUR

SHADES OF GOLD

SUMMARY OF PERFORMANCE

NAME_____ DATE_____

MULTIPLE-CHOICE ITEMS

VERY GOOD READER	AVERAGE READER	FAIR READER	POOR READER	PUPIL SCORE	COMMENTS
15-16	13-14	11-12	10 OR LESS	_____	_____

OPEN-ENDED ITEMS

EXCELLENT	ADEQUATE	UNSATISFACTORY	NONSCORABLE
3	2	1	NS

QUESTION 1   _____ _____

QUESTION 2   _____ _____

SELF-ASSESSMENT

COMMENTS   _____

_____

For permission to reprint copyrighted material, grateful acknowledgment is made to the following sources:

Highlights for Children, Inc., Columbus, OH: From "The Dragon That Munched" by Suzanne Burgoyne Dieckman in *Highlights for Children,* July/August 1986. Text copyright © 1986 by Highlights for Children, Inc.

Childrens Press, Inc.: From pp. 29–33 in *Guide Dog Winners* (Retitled: "Julie's Special Job") by Ed and Ruth Radlauer. Text copyright © 1983 by Childrens Press®, Inc.

Illustrations: Blanche Sims/Carol Bancroft & Friends—Artist's Representative, p. 3; Don Dyen/Philip M. Veloric—Artist's Representative, p. 7.

Printed in the United States of America

ISBN 0-15-305454-9

1 2 3 4 5 6 7 8 9 10   073   97   96   95   94

The Dragon That Munched

by Suzanne Burgoyne Dieckman

Directions: Read each story and the questions that follow. Fill in the answer circle in front of the correct answer for each question.

What was unusual about Roger's experimental computer?

"Ro-ger," his mother called up the stairs, "have you finished your homework?"

"I wish," said Roger to Dragon, "there was no such word as homework."

Actually, Roger didn't say that. He typed it on Dragon's keyboard. Dragon was a computer. A new, hush-hush, experimental model computer that Roger's dad (a very important scientist) was working on. Roger wasn't supposed to be playing with Dragon, of course. But his friend Charlie was a computer whiz, so Roger needed to practice to keep up.

The prompt **Do next?** appeared in green letters on Dragon's monitor.

Roger was getting a headache from concentrating so hard. Also, he was hungry.

Eat, he typed.

Eat what? replied Dragon.

Cookie, typed Roger.

Yum, printed Dragon. **Thank you.**

Roger turned off Dragon and went downstairs to the kitchen.

"Mom," he said, "may I have a nibblefritz?"

"What?" said his mother.

"I said, I'd like a chompsickle."

"What?"

No matter how hard Roger tried, he couldn't say the word *cookie*. Finally, he drew a picture.

Roger went back upstairs to Dragon.

Dragon, he typed, **did you eat the word** — Roger discovered he couldn't type *cookie*, either — **nummiewat?**

Yum, printed Dragon. **Eat next?**

Roger thought for a moment. Slowly, he typed into the computer, **homework**.

"Roger," his mother called up the stairs, "have you finished your thinkdoodle?"

"I'm doing it now, Mom," he yelled. He went to the phone and called his friend Charlie.

"Hey, Charlie, what are you doing?"

"I'm doing my memorpickle."

"That's what I thought," said Roger. "It can wait. Come over here. I've got something to show you."

Since Charlie lived next door, it wasn't long before he was standing next to Roger, blinking at Dragon's screen. "A computer that eats words? And after Dragon eats a word, nobody can say it? Hmm," he muttered. "What are you going to do?"

"Well," said Roger, "I was thinking of all the words I could feed to Dragon. Words I'd like to get rid of. Like *karate lessons*. I mean, my parents couldn't make me go, could they, if they couldn't say it?"

"I see what you mean," Charlie said. "But your vision is limited. Think big."

Before Roger could stop him, Charlie leaned over and typed **nuclear missile** after Dragon's **Eat next?** prompt.

Roger shook his head. He hurried to wash the dishes so he could watch the evening news.

"And the crisis of the hour," the newscaster was saying, "is the breakdown in the arms negotiation talks. At the special session tonight, negotiators on both sides found themselves unable to pronounce the words *bumbledy boomdoom*."

Roger ran for the phone. "Charlie," he whispered, "get over here. Fast. We're in trouble."

Harcourt Brace School Publishers • Unit Holistic Reading Assessment

Roger waited for Charlie to arrive before switching on Dragon.

"What do we do?" Roger demanded. "We've got to get him to give the words back."

Suddenly Roger sat down at the keyboard and began typing.

"What are you doing?" Charlie asked.

Chocolate fudge cake, typed Roger frantically. **Pistachio ice cream**. **Licorice sticks**.

Yum, printed Dragon. **Yum. Yum.**

Banana split. Coconut doughnut. Pizza with anchovies...

Yum, printed Dragon. **Yum.** All at once his letters flickered, like a hiccough. **Yuk.**

Dragon's monitor suddenly filled with words, spewing across the screen faster than Roger could read them. Roger took a deep breath and crossed his fingers. "Cookie," he said.

"How did you do that?" Charlie blinked in amazement.

Roger shrugged. "I just remembered what happened to *me* one time when I ate a lot of that stuff."

"You made Dragon upchuck all the words? By feeding him all that stuff?" Charlie blinked in disgust. "Yuk."

Go on

1. Dragon is _____ .

(A) Roger's nickname

(B) Roger's father's computer

(C) a new computer game

(D) the name of Roger's friend

2. Why was Roger using his dad's experimental computer?

(A) He wanted to learn how computers work.

(B) He had to do his homework.

(C) He wanted to keep up with his friend.

(D) He wanted to get a better grade in school.

3. In this story the word monitor means _____ .

(A) watch closely

(B) a computer screen

(C) follow directions

(D) a student helper

4. Roger's friend is _____ .

(A) very knowledgeable about computers

(B) the first one to finish the homework

(C) too busy to help him with his problem

(D) the one who got Roger into trouble

Harcourt Brace School Publishers • Unit Holistic Reading Assessment

Go on

5. The computer "ate" words whenever Roger or Charlie _____ .

    (A) said the words aloud

    (B) used nonsense words

    (C) turned it on

    (D) typed the words on the keyboard

6. Roger first realized what the computer was doing when _____ .

    (A) he couldn't say the word *cookie*

    (B) his mother asked him if he had finished his homework

    (C) the word *cookie* came up on the monitor

    (D) his friend told him

7. When Roger watched the news, he realized that _____ .

    (A) he had forgotten to finish his homework

    (B) he had missed his karate lessons

    (C) the computer made it impossible to use certain words

    (D) Charlie had played a trick on him

8. Roger figured out how to solve the problem by _____ .

    (A) reading the instruction manual

    (B) remembering something that had happened to him

    (C) finding out about a similar problem on the TV news

    (D) asking his father for advice

Name _____

Suppose you had a computer like Roger's. Write a paragraph telling how you would use your computer and what you would make it do.

_____

_____

_____

_____

_____

_____

_____

_____

_____

_____

_____

_____

_____

_____

_____

_____

_____

_____

Harcourt Brace School Publishers • Unit Holistic Reading Assessment

Julie's Special Job

by Ed and Ruth Radlauer

Why is Dad doing all the work?

[*Julie Brand has persuaded her parents to let her raise a golden retriever puppy that will later be trained as a guide dog for a blind person. Julie is to keep Goblin, the dog, for 15 months before turning her over to an organization named Guide Dogs of the Desert, which will train her.*]

One Sunday morning, Julie slept until 9 o'clock. When she got up and looked out the window, Dad had moved the doghouse onto the grass where he was hosing it out. The old blankets from inside the pup's house were hanging on the clothesline.

Dressing quickly, she ran out to the yard. "What are you doing, Dad?" she asked.

"Just all the stuff you promised to do." He sounded angry.

"Nobody said you had to clean house for a dog."

"How would you like to sleep in the same sheets for several weeks?"

It hardly seemed that important. "Come on, Goblin." She stomped back into the house. In her room she hugged the golden retriever. "Oh, Goblin, I

hope Dad doesn't make me send you back."

Goblin cocked her head to one side and whimpered with Julie. She burrowed her nose under Julie's hand, begging to be petted. "Besides," Julie told the pup, "you sleep in my room most of the time now anyway."

Julie began to feel better until she looked up to see Dad standing in the doorway. "I knew I'd end up doing all the work," he said.

Her shoulders sagged and she felt like crying. "But Dad, you move faster than anyone else in the house. You talk to *me* about patience—"

"What about it?"

She took a chance. "Well, you're not even <u>patient</u> enough to let other people do things at their own speed."

He started to answer, but kept quiet.

"Besides," she went on. "I think you *like* to do all the grooming and feeding. You never give *me* a chance to."

Dad sat down on the floor and rested his elbows on his knees. "You know, I think you're right."

"You do six things while the rest of us are thinking about one."

Dad's mad look went away. "I never got to have a dog when I was a kid. You know what Goblin did yesterday? She fetched the newspaper for me. How about that?"

"Dad, I *like* to <u>groom</u> and feed Goblin. She's calm and lovable when I groom her and not so jumpy and frustrating. And if you feed her all the time, she's going to love you more than she does me, and *I'm* supposed to be the puppy raiser."

"Hmmm. I guess you're trying to tell me to mind my own business and let you do your job, huh?" Dad stood up and gazed around the room. Looking disappointed, he dusted the edge of a bookshelf and pushed the books into an even row.

Julie smiled at him. "I don't mind if you groom or feed once in awhile."

"Okay," Dad said. "Just let me know when it's my turn — maybe when you have too much to do?"

"Dad?"

"Yes?"

"You love Goblin, too, don't you?"

He looked embarrassed. "Sure do," he admitted. "She's some dog!"

Go on ▷

9. This story is mainly about _____ .

- (A) how to raise a dog
- (B) a dog that gets into trouble
- (C) a girl and her father discussing their feelings
- (D) a girl who forgets to clean her room

10. In this story the word groom means _____ .

- (A) someone who takes care of horses
- (B) to brush and clean a dog's hair
- (C) a man who is getting married
- (D) to help someone get ready

11. In this story the word patient means _____ .

- (A) curious
- (B) willing to wait
- (C) stubborn
- (D) polite

12. Why does Dad act angry?

- (A) He thinks Julie is hiding from him.
- (B) He thinks the dog does not like him.
- (C) He is having to do Julie's work.
- (D) He does not like having a dog around.

13. How does Dad **really** feel about doing things for Goblin?

(A) He likes caring for her.

(B) He is too tired to care for her.

(C) He is upset about getting dirty.

(D) He feels tricked into all the work.

14. When she goes back to her room, Julie is worried that _____ .

(A) she has made Goblin sick

(B) the dog does not like her

(C) Dad might get rid of Goblin

(D) her room does not look tidy

15. Which sentence shows that Dad never gives Julie a chance to do her own work?

(A) Goblin cocked her head to one side and whimpered.

(B) Dad was cleaning the doghouse before Julie got up.

(C) Julie's shoulders sagged and she felt like crying.

(D) Dad never had a dog when he was young.

16. Which of these is a **fact** from the story?

(A) One Sunday morning Julie slept until 9 o'clock.

(B) I like to groom and feed Goblin.

(C) It hardly seemed that important.

(D) I hope Dad doesn't make me send you back.

Stop

Name _____

How does Dad feel about Goblin? Explain your reasons.

_____
_____
_____
_____
_____
_____
_____
_____
_____
_____
_____
_____
_____
_____
_____
_____
_____
_____
_____
_____

Name _____

Think about the selections you read in "Light Moments." Then complete this page. Underline the word or words in the first two items.

1. Did the selections remind you of things you have read before?

   Yes   I'm not sure   No

2. Would you choose these selections to read on your own?

   Yes   Maybe   No

3. Choose one selection that you might advise a friend to read. Write and explain why.

   _____

   _____

   _____

4. If you had a personal library, what kinds of literature would you include in it? List your choices.

   _____

   _____

   _____

5. List one or two things that made the selections in this unit easy or hard to enjoy and explain why.

   _____

   _____

   _____

6. Do these selections have enough action for you? Write a brief explanation of why or why not.

   _____

   _____

   _____

Harcourt Brace School Publishers • Unit Holistic Reading Assessment

TREASURY OF LITERATURE
SHADES OF GOLD
Unit Holistic Reading Assessment
Unit Four

HARCOURT
BRACE

Orlando Atlanta Austin Boston San Francisco Chicago Dallas New York
Toronto London

PART NO. 9997-09836-6

ISBN 0-15-305454-9 (12 OF EACH UNIT TEST)

Unit Holistic Reading Assessment
UNIT FIVE

SHADES OF GOLD

TREASURY OF LITERATURE

SUMMARY OF PERFORMANCE

NAME_____   DATE_____

MULTIPLE-CHOICE ITEMS

VERY GOOD READER	AVERAGE READER	FAIR READER	POOR READER	PUPIL SCORE	COMMENTS
15-16	13-14	11-12	10 OR LESS	- ___	_____

OPEN-ENDED ITEMS

EXCELLENT	ADEQUATE	UNSATISFACTORY	NONSCORABLE
3	2	1	NS

QUESTION 1   ___ _____

QUESTION 2   ___ _____

SELF-ASSESSMENT

COMMENTS   _____

_____

Illustrations: Len Ebert/Philip M. Veloric—Artist's Representative, p. 2; Don Dyen/Philip M. Veloric—Artist's Representative, p. 7, 8.

Printed in the United States of America

ISBN 0-15-305454-9

1 2 3 4 5 6 7 8 9 10   073   97   96   95   94

Nedu

Directions: Read each story and the questions that follow. Fill in the answer circle in front of the correct answer for each question.

How did Nedu escape drowning?

Nedu was still very young the winter that he asked his father if he could join the village fishermen in fishing for the yellow mullet, a small fish that travels in enormous groups. Nedu's people, the Imragen, were members of a small tribe who live in Mauritania, just north of the equator in western Africa. The Imragen have lived on the seashore for centuries, fishing with nets made from the fibers of desert plants. Over the years, they have learned that if they beat the waters with a board, dolphins will drive schools of fish into the shallow water where the Imragen can catch them in their nets.

Each winter, if it is a good season, many schools of fish move south, and the dolphins are there to drive them to shore. If the dolphins do not come, the fish pass by too far out to sea for the fishermen to catch them. The dolphins ensure the survival of the Imragen.

Nedu was an excellent swimmer, and he had often swum out far enough to find himself among a group of dolphins. He swam alongside them, sometimes holding onto the dorsal fin on a dolphin's back. The dolphins were his friends.

When Nedu asked his father about taking part in the winter fishing, his father just looked down at him. Nedu was young and wouldn't be much help to the fishermen, but his desire was clear. Father put his hand on the boy's shoulder and reminded him that he must not get in the way.

Harcourt Brace School Publishers • Unit Holistic Reading Assessment

Go on   1

Very early in the morning, the men huddled down among the dunes to escape the harsh sea wind. Standing like a statue, staring out at the sea and shading his eyes with his hand, Nedu seemed unaware of the cold. Soon, far out at sea, he saw a slight color change in the water. The yellow mullet were migrating south. A man rushed out to slap the water's surface with a board. Before long the dorsal fins of dolphins cut through the waves as they came toward the shore, driving the fish before them.

The men raised long poles draped with heavy nets to their shoulders. The nets were soon filled with thousands of fish, flinging themselves into the air and swimming at high speeds. The water boiled with leaping fish and dolphins swimming around the nets.

Nedu was so filled with awe that he had been unable to move. Suddenly he felt himself being pulled into the water as his foot became entangled, or caught, in one of the nets. Salty water rushed into his mouth. Almost at the same time, he felt the powerful body of a dolphin under his own. The force of the dolphin's movement freed his foot. Instinctively, as his body rolled over, he grabbed the dorsal fin on the dolphin's back and was pulled toward shore. As the water became shallow, the dolphin turned and swam out to sea, and Nedu stumbled onto the beach. For the rest of the morning, he watched the skillful fishermen as they dragged the heavy nets to the beach. Nedu was lost in his thoughts about the wonders of the partnership between his people and the dolphins. His own experience made him grateful to be part of it.

Go on

1. This story is mainly about _____ .

   (A) how dolphins survive in the sea
   (B) a beneficial partnership between a boy and a dolphin
   (C) the relationship between a boy and his father
   (D) how to use nets to catch schools of fish

2. The word mullet in the story refers to a type of _____ .

   (A) fiber
   (B) net
   (C) dolphin
   (D) fish

3. The word entangled in the story means _____ .

   (A) caught
   (B) involved
   (C) arranged
   (D) dragged

4. The word Imragen in the story refers to _____ .

   (A) Nedu's father's name
   (B) a seashore in western Africa
   (C) a tribe in Mauritania
   (D) the season for fishing

Harcourt Brace School Publishers • Unit Holistic Reading Assessment

Go on

5. One fisherman slapped the water with a board because it _____ .

Ⓐ scared the dolphins away so the men could catch the fish

Ⓑ made the dolphins drive the mullet toward the shore

Ⓒ stunned the fish into staying still

Ⓓ signaled to the fishermen to be ready with the nets

6. Far out at sea, Nedu saw a color change in the water because the _____ .

Ⓐ wind was blowing the water

Ⓑ man was beating the water with a board

Ⓒ yellow mullet were swimming in huge groups

Ⓓ sun was reflecting in the water

7. It is most likely that the dolphin that helped Nedu _____ .

Ⓐ was lost

Ⓑ didn't hear the sound of the board on the water

Ⓒ was trying to tear the nets

Ⓓ recognized him as a friend who had swum with him

8. Which lesson can best be learned from this story?

Ⓐ Men and animals can often work together.

Ⓑ If you want a job done right, do it yourself.

Ⓒ Young people should always listen to their elders.

Ⓓ It is impossible to control the forces of nature.

Harcourt Brace School Publishers • Unit Holistic Reading Assessment

Stop

Name _____

Explain why the dolphins are so important to the Imragen.

_____

_____

_____

_____

_____

_____

_____

_____

_____

_____

_____

_____

_____

_____

_____

_____

_____

_____

Harcourt Brace School Publishers • Unit Holistic Reading Assessment

Oceans

How much water is found on earth?

Water was once thought to be one of the four basic elements (Earth-Air-Fire-Water). Water covers approximately 70 percent of the earth's surface, or 139,434,000 square miles (388,755,999 square kilometers), while the land surface of the earth is only 57,506,000 square miles (148,940,540 square kilometers). There is just about the same amount of water on earth today as there was thousands of years ago.

Without water, our planet would be <u>uninhabitable</u>, or unfit to live in, because human beings, animals, and plants depend on water for life. It has been estimated that as many as nine out of ten organisms in the world live in the oceans.

While water covers 70 percent of the earth's surface, less than one percent is fresh water that we can drink. More than three-quarters of the fresh water along the earth's surface is frozen in the Antarctic ice cap.

The table on the next page provides some interesting statistics regarding the area and volume of water that is present on earth. Use the table to help answer the questions that follow this passage.

Go on

Harcourt Brace School Publishers • Unit Holistic Reading Assessment

THE VITAL STATISTICS OF

WATER

	Area* (square miles)	Volume* (cubic miles)	% of Total*
SALT WATER			
The oceans	139,500,000	317,000,000	97.2
Inland seas & saline (saltwater) lakes	270,000	25,000	0.008
FRESH WATER			
Freshwater lakes	330,000	30,000	0.009
All rivers (average level)		300	0.0001
Antarctic ice cap	6,000,000	6,300,000	1.9
Arctic ice cap & glaciers	900,000	680,000	0.15
Water in the atmosphere		3,100	0.001
GROUND WATER			
Surface		1,000,000	0.31
Deep-lying		1,000,000	0.31
TOTAL (approximate)		326,000,000	100.00

*All figures are estimated
Source: U.S. Department of the Interior

Harcourt Brace School Publishers • Unit Holistic Reading Assessment

Go on

9. According to the table, saline refers to water that is _____ .

   Ⓐ frozen
   Ⓑ fresh
   Ⓒ salty
   Ⓓ deep-lying

10. The word uninhabitable in the passage means _____ .

   Ⓐ very customary
   Ⓑ not suitable for plant or animal life
   Ⓒ lived in before
   Ⓓ sparsely populated by living beings

11. According to the table, all rivers on the earth combined make up _____ .

   Ⓐ 300 cubic miles
   Ⓑ 97 percent of the total water
   Ⓒ 30,000 cubic miles
   Ⓓ 900,000 square miles

12. Cubic miles are used in the table to show water's _____ .

   Ⓐ quality
   Ⓑ temperature
   Ⓒ depth
   Ⓓ volume

13. The total volume of water on the earth is _____ .

(A) 326,000,000 cubic miles

(B) 139,500,000 square miles

(C) 317,000,000 cubic miles

(D) 147,000,000 square miles

14. According to the passage, about ninety percent of the world's organisms live in _____ .

(A) the Arctic

(B) glaciers

(C) the oceans

(D) fresh water

15. The Antarctic ice cap has more than three-quarters of the earth's _____ .

(A) glaciers

(B) fresh water

(C) atmospheric water

(D) salt water

16. The way information is presented in this passage shows _____ .

(A) general facts and statistics on a subject

(B) causes of a particular event

(C) reasons to support a point of view

(D) the order in which things happened

Stop

Name _____

Based on what you read in this passage, explain why most of the
earth's water cannot be used for drinking.

_____

_____

_____

_____

_____

_____

_____

_____

_____

_____

_____

_____

_____

_____

_____

_____

_____

_____

Stop

Name _____

Think about the selections you read in "Oceans." Then complete this page. Underline the word or words in the first two items.

1. Did you have trouble keeping your mind on these selections?

   Not often   Sometimes   Often

2. Would you like to read more selections like these?

   Yes   Maybe   No

3. Write a brief explanation about why you do or do not like the type of selections in this unit.

   _____

   _____

   _____

4. In what ways have your reading interests changed as a result of reading the selections in this unit? List some of them.

   _____

   _____

   _____

5. Do you think you will remember these selections for a long time? Explain why or why not.

   _____

   _____

   _____

6. Write about the most interesting thing you learned in this unit.

   _____

   _____

   _____

Harcourt Brace School Publishers • Unit Holistic Reading Assessment

TREASURY OF LITERATURE
SHADES OF GOLD
Unit Holistic Reading Assessment
Unit Five

HARCOURT
BRACE

Orlando Atlanta Austin Boston San Francisco Chicago Dallas New York
Toronto London

PART NO. 9997-09837-4

ISBN 0-15-305454-9 (12 OF EACH UNIT TEST)

TREASURY OF LITERATURE

UNIT HOLISTIC
READING ASSESSMENT
UNIT SIX

SHADES OF GOLD

SUMMARY OF PERFORMANCE

NAME_____   DATE_____

MULTIPLE-CHOICE ITEMS

VERY GOOD READER	AVERAGE READER	FAIR READER	POOR READER	PUPIL SCORE	COMMENTS
15-16	13-14	11-12	10 OR LESS	_____	_____

OPEN-ENDED ITEMS

EXCELLENT	ADEQUATE	UNSATISFACTORY	NONSCORABLE
3	2	1	NS

QUESTION 1   _____   _____

QUESTION 2   _____   _____

SELF-ASSESSMENT

COMMENTS   _____

_____

Illustrations: Don Dyen/Philip M. Veloric—Artist's Representative, p. 1, 8.

Printed in the United States of America

ISBN 0-15-305454-9

1 2 3 4 5 6 7 8 9 10   073   97   96   95   94

Into the Past

Directions: Read each story and the questions that follow. Fill in the answer circle in front of the correct answer for each question.

What kind of town did Tim visit?

Tim was exhausted. For three weeks he and his parents had been camping along the coast of Maine. He could hardly wait to get home and hug Chipper, his dog. He wanted to sit out on their deck and drink cold milk. Then he would watch TV before going up to sleep in his own bed.

His dad turned off the highway onto a side road, intending to stop at a clothing factory Mother wanted to visit.

"Oh, oh!" Tim's dad said, pulling the car over.

"Detour," his mom read from a sign. Tim sighed. A detour always made him feel so uncomfortable. Instead of seeming like an unexpected adventure, it always seemed <u>foreboding</u> somehow, like a warning.

His dad followed the detour sign down an unpaved road. For nearly a hour, they saw no cars or people. Finally they drove into a little town where people were milling around outside. "How charming!" Mother said. "They're all in costumes that look at least 150 years old!" All their houses seemed quite old and quaint, too. Some were log cabins.

The people stared in amazement at Tim and his family. As Tim's dad pulled the car over, a crowd gathered around. Yet many people stood back, some distance away. The women stared at Tim's mother, who looked a bit conspicuous in her slacks. Lots of people leaned forward, staring at the car.

NOWHERE
POPULATION 112

"Where's your horse?" someone in the crowd called out. Dad thought it was a wonderful joke and laughed out loud. Tim couldn't help noticing that there were no other cars in sight.

Two boys at the edge of the crowd started waving at him. "Patrick!" they called. "Where in tarnation have you been? We thought you went bear hunting and got lost!" Tim couldn't convince the boys that his name was not Patrick. He began answering to the name and soon became friends with the boys and felt right at home.

Tim's mother noticed some interesting stores and decided to do some shopping. What a wonderful day she had! No one would accept her money, so she bartered by trading things she had with her for things made by women in the town. Tim's dad went through the shops where candles and saddles were made and saw one where horses were shoed.

When it came time to leave, Father asked the way to Philadelphia. Everyone found this amusing, since there was only the one road in and out of the town.

"You're not going off again?" one of the boys asked Tim. The boys clung to the open windows of the car, talking to Tim inside. They recoiled very quickly, however, at the sound of the car's engine.

"So long again, Patrick," Tim heard one boy call out as Father began to drive away. Tim looked back and saw a hand-painted sign that said, "Nowhere. Population 112."

"Their act is very convincing," Tim's father said. "They even have calendars that say 1814. I'm surprised they don't attract more tourists."

"You know," Tim's mother said, "they had just finished making this jam — but the date on the jar label says 1814! Aren't they clever!"

Tim settled back for a long ride, but all at once they rounded a corner, and there was the highway right outside their hometown!

Tim yawned, wondering how it had gotten dark so fast. Inside their house, Chipper jumped up to greet him. Tim gave Chipper a hug; then he went to the desk and took out a map. He studied the map carefully for several minutes — but he could not find "Nowhere" on it anywhere.

1. This story is mostly about a boy and his family who _____ .

    Ⓐ spend a wonderful day shopping with friends
    Ⓑ follow a detour that leads them back in time
    Ⓒ see no cars or people after they take a detour
    Ⓓ go camping along the coast of Maine

2. This story could best be described as a _____ .

    Ⓐ scientific report
    Ⓑ news article
    Ⓒ comedy
    Ⓓ science fiction story

3. The word foreboding in the story means _____ .

    Ⓐ predicting bad things in advance
    Ⓑ giving extra signs
    Ⓒ staying without permission
    Ⓓ waiting again

4. The word bartered in the story means _____ .

    Ⓐ worked
    Ⓑ left
    Ⓒ exchanged
    Ⓓ begged

5. The words in the story that help you know what <u>bartered</u> means are _____ .

- (A) everyone laughed
- (B) by trading things
- (C) started waving at him
- (D) leaned forward

6. The author of this story wants readers to think that the town is _____ .

- (A) strange
- (B) modern
- (C) unfriendly
- (D) dangerous

7. The author says that "Nowhere" is not on a map in order to show that the town is _____ .

- (A) in a foreign country
- (B) a tourist attraction
- (C) not a real place
- (D) Tim's hometown

8. Which question is **not** answered in the story?

- (A) Why did the detour seem to result in a time change?
- (B) Where were Tim and his parents at the end of the story?
- (C) What was unusual about Mother's jar of jam?
- (D) Where had the family spent their vacation earlier?

ourt Brace School Publishers • Unit Holistic Reading Assessment

Stop

Name _____

Think about the clues the author provided in the story. Then write some of the clues the author gave to make readers think it really *was* 1814 in the town of Nowhere.

_____

_____

_____

_____

_____

_____

_____

_____

_____

_____

_____

_____

_____

_____

_____

_____

_____

_____

Stop

The Pony Express

What was the pony express, and what caused it to end?

Getting mail to the Far West was a difficult and time-consuming task in 1860. Stagecoaches took four weeks or more to make the run from Missouri to California. To speed up the mail, a pony service that included 190 stations manned with 400 keepers and helpers was initiated. The first run — made on April 14, 1860 — covered 1,966 miles over the desert and mountains from the western end of the railway at St. Joseph, Missouri, to Sacramento, California. It required ten and one-half days and forty riders.

The company that established the pony express bought 400 fast ponies and hired a team of eighty expert riders. They traveled more than ten miles an hour over mountains and up to twenty-five miles an hour on flat stretches. The riders stayed on one pony for ten to fifteen miles, then changed mounts and rode at top speed to the next relay station.

The keeper would run out with a fresh mount as the rider approached and sounded a little horn he carried with him. The rider jumped from his mount, threw his pouch on the new pony, and sped away within two minutes. The pouch was a waterproof leather bag that never weighed more than twenty pounds. Since every ounce was a drag on the horse, the riders had to weigh under 125 pounds; and they carried only what they needed — horn, pistol, and knife — to defend themselves against attack. Not even a water jug was allowed to add to the load.

It cost five dollars to send a one-half ounce letter by the pony line. That was a lot of money in those days; but despite some complaints, the need was so great that the service had to be doubled from once a week to twice a week. Most writers used thin writing paper and wrote as few words as possible.

Harcourt Brace School Publishers • Unit Holistic Reading Assessment

Go on

The riders — all teenagers — faced many dangers as they raced across the western lands. The course was not clearly marked. There was always the danger of enemy attack over the lonely stretches of land. In winter, hungry wolf packs ran across the route, and in the high country there were mountain lions. But records show that in 650,000 miles covered, only one mailbag was ever lost.

The pony riders earned from $100 to $150 a month — very good wages for that time. Their uniform of buckskin jacket, red shirt, bright blue jeans, and black boots made them colorful figures of the time. While the average rider's age was eighteen, some were hired as young as fifteen. They rode as much as eighteen hours a day, riding in rain, snow, or burning desert sun, catching a short nap, then riding on again. The ponies they rode were chosen for speed, courage, and endurance, and were considered to be the finest in the West.

As the danger of the Civil War was foreseen, telegraph lines were pushed rapidly across the country. The wire service began in 1861. It spelled the decline and eventual end of the pony express. The telegraph handled messages more quickly and cheaply. The pony express came to an end eighteen months after it had begun.

Go on

9. Before the pony express, mail was delivered by _____ .

   Ⓐ boat
   Ⓑ railroad
   Ⓒ stagecoach
   Ⓓ telegraph lines

10. Young men probably most wanted to serve as pony express riders because the _____ .

   Ⓐ job was safe
   Ⓑ pay was good
   Ⓒ hours were short
   Ⓓ horses were gentle

11. One requirement for being a pony express rider involved _____ .

   Ⓐ weight
   Ⓑ height
   Ⓒ education
   Ⓓ experience

12. Pony express riders could best be described as _____ .

   Ⓐ curious
   Ⓑ lucky
   Ⓒ brave
   Ⓓ smart

13. The pony express service ended because _____ .

   Ⓐ there were not enough riders
   Ⓑ telegraph service began
   Ⓒ people could not afford the service
   Ⓓ there was no need for mail during the Civil War

14. Which sentence shows best that the pony express delivery record was good?

(A) Only one mailbag was ever lost.

(B) They made it in ten and one-half days.

(C) They only needed eighty riders.

(D) It cost five dollars to send a one-half ounce letter.

15. There is enough information in the passage to believe that the pony express was _____ .

(A) ineffective because of the high cost

(B) unnecessary, but a colorful part of the Old West

(C) better than the telegraph service that took its place

(D) fast, efficient, and served the needs of the time

16. Which sentence best sums up the ideas in the passage?

(A) The pony express failed to meet the needs of the public and was disbanded six months after it began.

(B) The pony express was started to speed up mail delivery to the Far West, and it ended when telegraph service went into effect.

(C) The pony express was a cheap and efficient method of delivering mail to the Far West.

(D) The pony express was an efficient method of mail delivery that took the place of telegraph service in the West.

Harcourt Brace School Publishers • Unit Holistic Reading Assessment

Stop

Name _____

Write a paragraph describing the ideal pony express rider.

_____

_____

_____

_____

_____

_____

_____

_____

_____

_____

_____

_____

_____

_____

_____

_____

_____

_____

_____

Harcourt Brace School Publishers • Unit Holistic Reading Assessment

Name _____

Think about the selections you read in "Other Places." Then complete this page. Underline the word or words in the first two items.

1. As you read the selections in this unit, did you picture events and characters in your mind?
    Yes   Sometimes   No

2. How easy or hard were the selections in this unit to read?
    Most were easy.   Most were hard.   All were hard.

3. Write about one or two things that made the selections in this unit easy or hard to enjoy and explain why.

    _____

    _____

    _____

4. List some ways in which you have become a more successful reader this year.

    _____

    _____

    _____

5. Are the selections in this unit the kind that you most like to read? Write a brief explanation telling why or why not.

    _____

    _____

    _____

6. Write about the most interesting thing that you learned in this unit.

    _____

    _____

    _____

Harcourt Brace School Publishers • Unit Holistic Reading Assessment

TREASURY OF LITERATURE

SHADES OF GOLD

UNIT HOLISTIC READING ASSESSMENT
UNIT SIX

HARCOURT
BRACE

Orlando Atlanta Austin Boston San Francisco Chicago Dallas New York
Toronto London

PART NO. 9997-09838-2

ISBN 0-15-305454-9 (12 OF EACH UNIT TEST)

6

LIMITED LOAN

DATE DUE

DEMCO, INC. 38-2931